Hybrid Vehicle Propulsion

International Series on Advances in Transport

Objectives

The objective of this Series is to provide state-of-the-art information on all aspects of transport research and applications. This covers land, water and air systems with emphasis on multi-mode operation. The books in the Series deal with planning operation and management as well as engineering aspects of transport. Environmental topics and sustainability are an important part of the Series. City, national and international transport are covered and encompassing interdisciplinary aspects.

Transport strategies
Planning and funding
Transport and economic issues
Operations and management
Private and public initiatives and policies
Regulation and standardisation
Transport and land use planning
Sustainable transport
Environmental issues
Information technology and electronic aspects
Multi-media and advanced training techniques
Management information systems
Human interface and decision support
Traveller psychology and behaviour
Emerging technologies
Transport and energy
Air transportation

Railway systems
Water and sea transport
Road transport
Urban transport systems
Terminal and interchanges
People movers
Multi-mode systems
Traffic integration
Infrastructure
Scheduling and traffic control
Vehicle technology
Safety and accident prevention
Hazardous transport risk
Hazardous remediation
Transport in extreme conditions
Freight transport

Associate Editors

Hybrid Vehicle Propulsion

C.M. Jefferson
University of the West of England, Bristol, UK

R.H. Barnard
University of Hertfordshire, UK

WITPRESS Southampton, Boston

C.M. Jefferson
University of the West of England, Bristol, UK

R.H. Barnard
University of Hertfordshire, UK

Published by

WIT Press
Ashurst Lodge, Ashurst, Southampton, SO40 7AA, UK
Tel: 44 (0) 238 029 3223; Fax: 44 (0) 238 029 2853
E-Mail: witpress@witpress.com
http://www.witpress.com

For USA, Canada and Mexico

Computational Mechanics Inc
25 Bridge Street, Billerica, MA 01821, USA
Tel: 978 667 5841; Fax: 978 667 7582
E-Mail: info@compmech.com
US site: http://www.compmech.com

British Library Cataloguing-in-Publication Data

A Catalogue record for this book is available
from the British Library

ISBN: 1-85312-887-2
ISSN: 1462-608X

Library of Congress Catalog Card Number: 2002106152

Printed in Great Britain by IBT Global Ltd, London.

Cover picture: Phileas hybrid electric bus, photo by Colin Brader, Integrated Transport
Planning Ltd.

Preface

The development of hybrid vehicles is probably one of the most significant advances in automotive technology in recent decades. It has been spurred on by a pressing requirement for the reduction in the environmental impact of land transport, particularly urban transport. Until recently, the electric vehicle was seen as the panacea for such problems, but the limited and insufficient development of batteries has turned attention to alternative solutions. The fuel cell car has become something of a new Holy Grail, but if this is a solution at all, it is likely to be in the long term. For the short and medium term, hybrid vehicles can combine the best features of existing automotive technology with the latest developments in power electronic converters and energy storage devices.

The term 'hybrid' implies the bringing together of two forms of vehicle propulsion, normally mechanical and electrical, drawing on the best features of each, to produce a vehicle which not only meets user needs, but also can comply with increasingly demanding environmental standards. Even if fuel cell vehicles do eventually come into widespread use, they are likely to employ a hybrid approach, with the fuel cell being supplemented by a storage system to provide boost power and regenerative braking.

The hybrid vehicle is just coming of age, and the first generation of hybrid cars is now available to the general public. Hybrid buses and trolleybuses have already entered regular service. The publication of this book is thus timely.

In the book, we review recent progress in the development of a range of hybrid vehicles, from small cars to buses and light rail vehicles. In the final chapter we describe the results of field trials and operational experience.

The authors
2002

Foreword

The Hybrid Propulsion System Research and Development Community: An Appreciation

For several years, one of the authors of this book, Colin Jefferson, has been actively involved in research on hybrid propulsion systems. During this period, he has had the privilege of working with some of the leading figures in the development of hybrid propulsion systems for public transport vehicles. A great deal of important pioneering work on light rail vehicle propulsion systems was carried out on a European Union funded project named ULEV-TAP, in which Dr Jefferson was involved. The results were presented at the PROSPER congress in Karlsruhe in September 2001, and the authors would like to acknowledge the work of partners and colleagues in that project, in particular:

Professor Colin Besant and Dr Shahram Etemad of Imperial College London, for their tireless work in seeing the project through and their contribution of gas turbine alternator design,

Joachim Berndt and Andreas Lohner of Kiepe Elektrik, Düsseldorf for their contribution to electrical design and integration,

Serge Bertrand, Wolfgang Glebe, Pascal Geoffroy and the staff of Alstom DDF, Reichshoffen for their contribution to mechanical integration and project leadership,

Jean Divoux and Claire Demartini of Turbomeca, Tarbes, and Professor Kyriakos Papaliou of the National Technical University of Athens, for their contribution on gas turbine design and implementation,

Terry Davies, Mike Ackerman and José Mauro Marquez of the University of the West of England, with whom Dr Jefferson worked on vehicle simulation,

Manuel Rocha Teixeira of STCP Porto, for his advice on operator requirements,

Dr Frans Thoolen and the staff of CCM, Nuenen, Netherlands, who have undertaken such pioneering work in flywheel energy storage system design over the last decade.

Axel Kühn, Nils Jänig and Johan van Ieperen at Transport Technologie-consult Karlsruhe for their dedicated work in promoting the application of hybrid propulsion in light rail transport. This culminated in the organisation of the PROSPER congress in Karlsruhe in September 2001, which brought together the leading players in the development of hybrid passenger transit vehicles from around the world. Much of the text, particularly that presented in Chapter 7, draws on the proceedings of this congress. It is anticipated that this congress will have stimulated interest in the deployment and further development of hybrid technology in passenger transit systems.

In addition to the collaborators on the ULEV-TAP project, the authors would like to acknowledge the pioneering work of John Parry of Parry People Movers, who has developed a range of innovative ultra light rail vehicles referred to in this book. Again, Dr Jefferson is grateful for having been associated with some of this work.

James Skinner of Bristol Electric Railbus and Bristol City Council have made an important contribution with their pioneering work in demonstrating the Parry ultra light rail vehicle on Bristol Harbourside between 1998 and 2001. This provided valuable operating experience of flywheel powered vehicles.

Antonio Vicente y Silva of the company Eletra in Brazil has made a major contribution to the development of what are probably the most successful hybrid electric buses in the world thus far.

C.M. Jefferson,
2002

Acknowledgements

Thanks are due to the companies CCM, Magnet Motor, APT and Eletra for the supply of photographs and permission to use them. Thanks are also due to Adriano Alessandrini and Luca Persia, Ingegneria dei Trasporti S.r.l., Frans Thoolen of CCM, Gerhard Reiner of Magnet Motor, Antonio Vicente y Silva of Eletra, and Ruud Bouwman of APTS, for permission to draw on the material in their papers presented at the PROSPER congress.

Photographs that are not attributed are by the authors.

Glossary of Terms

Adiabatic expansion	Expansion of a gas with no heat transfer.
Aerodynamic drag	Retarding force due to air resistance.
Alcohol	As fuel, usually methanol or ethanol.
Alternator	Rotating machine acting as electrical generator or motor.
Anode	Negative electrode of a battery or fuel cell.
Auxiliaries	Vehicle components, apart from main drive, requiring power supply, such as lights and air-conditioning.
Brake energy	Energy absorbed in retarding the vehicle, mainly by the brakes in a conventional vehicle.
Brayton cycle	Thermodynamic cycle in which heat addition and rejection takes place at constant pressure, as in a gas turbine.
Capacitor	Passive device for storing electrical charge and therefore energy.
Cardanic suspension	Gimballed suspension of flywheel.
Carnot cycle	Thermodynamic cycle in which heat addition and rejection takes place at constant temperature, as in a Stirling engine.
Catalyst	Passive element to promote a chemical reaction.
Catalytic converter	Device for rendering pollutant emissions harmless by chemical reactions promoted by a catalyst.
Cathode	Positive electrode of battery or fuel cell.
Combined cycle	A combination of two or more types of thermodynamic cycle.
Converter	Power electronic device for converting electrical power DC to AC or vice versa.
Cryogenic storage	Storage at very low temperatures
Cycle life	The number of charge/discharge cycles that an energy storage device can withstand during its life.
DC link	The usual form of electrical power transmission between converters.
Diesel generator set	Electrical generator powered by a diesel engine.
Drag coefficient	Dimensionless factor relating to the aerodynamic drag, and associated with the shape of the vehicle.
Dump resistors	An electrical means of dissipating excess brake energy.
Efficiency	Output power / input power, normally as %.

Efficiency contour	Contour of uniform % efficiency in an efficiency map.
Elastic polymer	Compressible material used in hydraulic accumulators.
Emissions	Normally from vehicle, measured in grams/km or grams/hour.
Energy density	Energy storage capacity per unit volume, kJ/litre.
Energy storage unit	A device for storing energy such as a battery.
Epicyclic gear	A type of gear train employing a central sun gear with a ring of planet gears and an outer gear ring.
Error	Difference between demand value and actual value.
Excitation	Generation of magnetic field in an electrical machine on no load.
External combustion	Combustion of the fuel which takes place outside the working cylinder or chamber.
Flywheel	High speed high inertia wheel able to store energy in the short term.
Fuel cell	Device for reacting hydrogen with oxygen to produce electrical power.
Fuel efficiency	Popular term meaning the distance travelled per litre of fuel.
Greenhouse effect	The tendency of the upper atmosphere to retain heat absorbed from sunlight.
Greenhouse gases	Gaseous emissions which contribute to the greenhouse effect.
Hydraulic accumulator	A means of storing energy using the energy of compression of elastic objects held in a cylinder of liquid.
Induction motor	Motor driven by (electronically controlled) rotating magnetic field.
Integral control	Control action which accumulates over time.
Internal combustion engine	Engine in which combustion of the fuel takes place in the working cylinder or chamber, as in a reciprocating petrol, gas or diesel engine.
Joule	Unit of energy = 1 Watt second.
Kinetic energy	Energy due to movement ($= 1/2$ mass $\times$ speed^2).
Kyoto protocol	International agreement on greenhouse gas emissions, proposed at Kyoto in 1997.
Mechanical variator	Mechanical transmission with continuously variable ratio.
Micron	One millionth of a metre.
Mild hybrid, mybrid	Hybrid with a small proportion of energy storage.
Motor/generator	Electrical machine able to act as motor or generator.
Octane rating	A measure of fuel ignition properties.
Otto cycle	Thermodynamic cycle in which heat addition and rejection take place at a constant volume, as in a petrol engine.
Parallel hybrid	Hybrid system where there is a direct mechanical transmission between the prime-mover engine and the wheels.

Part load	Condition of engine running at well below its rated power.
Petrol (UK)	Gasoline (USA).
Pollution concentration	Atmospheric pollution measured in micrograms per m^3.
Power density	Power rating per unit volume, W/litre.
Pressure induced ignition	Mechanism for ignition in diesel engines.
Prime mover	The main continuous power source.
Rankine cycle	Thermodynamic cycle using vapour produced by heating a liquid.
Reformer (Hydrogen)	Means of producing hydrogen from other fuels.
Regenerative braking	Reversal of the transmission power flow to retard the vehicle and recharge the stored energy device.
Rolling resistance	Retarding force on vehicle due to resistance of the wheels to rolling on road.
Rolling resistance coeff.	Dimensionless coefficient relating the resistance to motion provided by the wheels to the vehicle weight.
Reciprocating engine	Normally engines with reciprocating pistons.
Recuperator	Means of recycling exhaust heat in a gas turbine.
Self-discharge	Tendency for an energy storage device to discharge itself over a period of time.
Series hybrid	Normally electrical transmission throughout.
Solid polymer	Insulating material used in ultracapacitors.
Spark ignition engine	Engines, such as petrol (gasoline), in which the fuel is ignited by an electrical spark.
Specific energy	Energy storage capacity per unit mass, kJ/kg.
Specific power	Power rating per unit mass, W/kg.
Speed profile	Variation of speed with time.
Stirling engine	Type of external combustion heat engine.
Storage efficiency	Energy output / energy input (%).
Transmission efficiency	Power at wheels/input power to transmission (%).
Torque splitting	A means of proportioning the power inputs from two or more sources.
Trolleybus	Bus running on an electrical overhead wire supply collected by a pair of 'trolley' masts.
Turbocharger	Means of increasing the air pressure at intake in a reciprocating engine by using a turbine driven by the exhaust gases.
Ultracapacitor	Capacitor with high energy storage capacity.
Ultra light rail	A form of light rail transport using small vehicles and no overhead supply.
Voltage converter	Power electronic device for converting from one DC voltage to another.

Nomenclature

a	Acceleration	(m/s^2)
A	Frontal area	(m^2)
C_D	Drag coefficient	
D	Aerodynamic drag	(N)
F_b	Braking force at the road	(N)
F_r	Rolling resistance	(N)
k_r	Rolling resistance coefficient	
m	Mass	(kg)
P	Power	(kW)
ρ	Density of air	(kg/m^3)
t	time	(s)
V	Vehicle speed	(m/s)
W	Weight	(N)

Abbreviations

AC	Alternating current.
ALABC	Advanced Lead Acid Battery Consortium.
BEV	Battery electric vehicle.
C1	Discharge time of 1 hour (batteries).
C5	Discharge time of 5 hours (batteries).
CCM	Research and development company in Netherlands which developed EMAFER.
CNG	Compressed natural gas.
CO	Carbon monoxide, toxic gas.
CO_2	Carbon dioxide, main product of combustion.
CVT	Continuously variable transmission (variator), alternative to gearbox.
DC	Direct current.
DOD	Depth of discharge (batteries).
EMAFER	Electro mechanical accumulator for energy recuperation.
EURO	EURO I-V emission standards for vehicles.
F	Farad, unit of electrical capacitance.
g/km	Grams per kilometre.
HC	Hydrocarbon compounds, possible pollutant and health hazard.
HEV	Hybrid electric vehicle
HGV	Heavy Goods Vehicle.
HOV	High occupancy vehicle.
i.c.	Internal combustion (engine).
IGBT	Insulated gate bipolar transistor.
IMA	Integrated motor assist.
kJ	Kilo Joule, unit of energy = 1000 Joules.
kWh	KiloWatt hour, unit of energy = 3600 kJ.
LEV	Low emission vehicle
LPG	Liquefied petroleum gas, usually butane.
MDS	Magnetodynamic storage.
MJ	Mega Joule, unit of energy = 1,000,000 Joules
Ni-Cd	Nickel cadmium (battery).
NiMH	Nickel metal-hydride (battery).

NOx	Oxides of nitrogen, NO, NO_2, pollutants and health hazard.
NSCA	National Society for Clean Air.
P + I	Proportional + integral control.
PEM	Proton exchange membrane.
PM	Particulate matter emitted into the atmosphere.
PM_{10}	Particulate matter comprising particles 10 microns in diameter or less.
$PM_{2.5}$	Particulate matter comprising particles 2.5 microns in diameter or less.
PNGV	Partnership for a New Generation of Vehicles.
SOx	Oxides of sulphur: pollutants and health hazard.
S.I.	Système International: standard for metric units.
SIMTRIP	Computer model used for performance simulation.
THS	Toyota hybrid system.
THS-M	Toyota hybrid system-mild.
ULEV	Ultra low emission vehicle.
ULEV-TAP	Ultra Low Emission Vehicle-Transport with Advanced Propulsion (European project).
UK	United Kingdom of Great Britain and Northern Ireland.
USABC	US Advanced Battery Consortium.
USCAR	US Council for Automotive Research.
Wh	Watt hour, = 3600 Joules.
V	Volts.
ZEV	Zero emission vehicle.
VOC	Volatile organic compound (s), pollutant and health hazard.

Contents

Chapter 1

WHY HYBRID?

Hybrid propulsion systems provide a means of improving the fuel efficiency and reducing the emissions of most forms of land transport. Such improvements will be beneficial on a number of counts, including;

1. reducing the cost of transportation
2. reducing the rate of depletion of fossil fuels
3. reducing the level of atmospheric pollutants, particularly in urban areas
4. reducing the build up of so-called 'greenhouse' gases.

In addition, depending on the particular hybrid arrangement, there are additional benefits, including quieter operation, the ability to operate in zero emissions mode for short distances, and stepless transmission.

1.1 The hybrid vehicle concept

A hybrid vehicle may be defined conveniently as a vehicle having two power sources. Usually, one of these sources derives its power from fuel, whilst the other relies on stored energy which can be used for extra power at various stages during a journey. The stored energy may also be replenished by the fuelled power source, or by recovering energy that would normally be lost in braking.

The concept of the hybrid motor vehicle is almost as old as the motor car itself. In 1905 an American engineer H. Piper filed a patent for a vehicle propelled by a combination of a petrol (gasoline) engine and an electric motor. The purpose of this arrangement was to enhance the performance of the vehicle, since internal combustion engines at the time had a very poor power to weight ratio.

In recent times, various forms of hybrid vehicles have emerged. These range from vehicles which are effectively battery electric vehicles (BEV) with a small internal combustion engine to recharge the battery, to almost conventional vehicles which incorporate an added electric traction motor and a small amount of energy storage. The latter type is commonly known as a 'mild hybrid' or 'mybrid', and represents a means of improving the efficiency of conventionally powered vehicles. A detailed explanation of how the hybrid propulsion arrangement produces this improvement is given later, but essentially, by using a hybrid system, a considerably smaller main engine can be used than in the corresponding conventional vehicle. This is because only a fraction of the maximum engine power is normally used for the greater part of any journey, and the short bursts of high power needed for acceleration and hill climbing can be provided from stored energy. The provision of a limited amount of energy storage capacity also enables the energy that would normally be lost in braking to be stored and later released.

There is no commonly accepted name for the other type of hybrid (the BEV with on-board recharging), and we will refer to it as a 'large energy storage hybrid'. The provision of a large amount of stored energy allows this type of vehicle to be used predominantly as a zero emission vehicle, whilst allowing it to make extended trips by using the engine to top up some of the energy taken from the battery.

The advantages of the hybrid arrangement can be understood by considering the behaviour of a hybrid propulsion system during a simple, short, start/stop journey cycle. Figure 1.1 shows the ideal speed and power history for a typical light rail vehicle for such a journey.

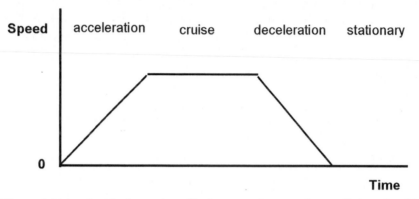

Figure 1.1(a): An ideal speed profile for a stop/start cycle on a light rail vehicle.

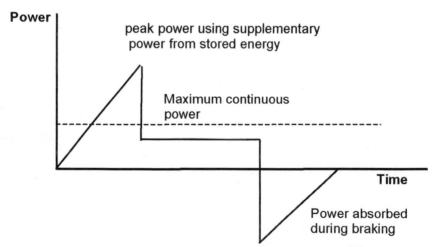

Figure 1.1(b): Corresponding theoretical power demand by the propulsion system.

For reasons of passenger comfort, the vehicle is designed to accelerate and decelerate at a constant rate. The upper diagram, figure 1.1(a) shows the speed history, and the lower one, figure 1.1(b) shows the power required.

From the power curve it may be seen that high power is only used for a very small part of the journey. In a mild hybrid vehicle, the primary motor is sized so that its power is at least adequate for cruise, as indicated by the dotted line. In large energy storage hybrids this may not be the case, and the stored energy will be gradually reduced. During acceleration, the additional power required for acceleration is taken from the stored energy device.

Figure 1.2(a) illustrates schematically the behaviour of a hybrid arrangement during the acceleration phase. The smaller engine has to work at a more constant power setting, and at a higher percentage of its maximum power than the large engine that it replaces. In the case of internal combustion engines, this greatly improves the efficiency. Spark-ignition engines have a particularly poor part-load efficiency.

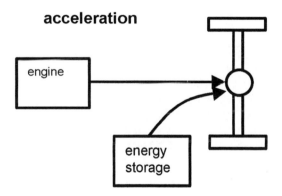

acceleration

Figure 1.2(a):   The hybrid arrangement during the acceleration phase. Additional power is provided by the storage device.

During the cruise phase, some spare power capacity in the main power source is used to top up the energy in the storage device, as illustrated in figure 1.2(b).

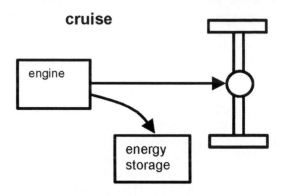

Figure 1.2(b):   The hybrid arrangement during the cruise phase. Excess energy
                  can be used to recharge the storage device.

It can be seen from figure 1.1, that during deceleration, the power requirement
is negative. That is, energy has to be absorbed by the braking system. In a hybrid
vehicle, instead of just dissipating this energy as heat in the braking system, the
energy storage device can be used to absorb and recycle it. The fuel consumption
is thus reduced. In a system using a battery as the storage device, the wheels are
mechanically connected to an electrical generator which supplies current to
recharge the storage unit and at the same time provides a braking resistance load
to the wheels. This phase is illustrated in figure 1.2(c).

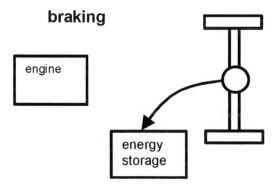

Figure 1.2(c):   The braking phase. Energy is fed back into the storage device.

There are some subsidiary benefits of the hybrid arrangement, including the possibility of using the stored energy to rapidly restart the main engine which can thus be switched off during periods of inactivity; for instance, in traffic jams.

As will be shown, the hybrid propulsion system can be applied using almost any combination of primary power supply and energy storage device. The first generation of production domestic cars used a combination of internal combustion engine and electric battery but, as will be discussed later, this is unlikely to be the preferred arrangement in the long term.

1.2 Hybrid vehicles and the environment

The hybrid propulsion system can be of benefit to the environment on two fronts.

1. At a global level, it can help to reduce the emissions of greenhouse gases, by providing more energy efficient transportation.
2   At a local level, particularly in urban areas, it can reduce the amount of other gases such as the oxides of nitrogen that are harmful both to the environment, and to human health.

It will be shown later that the hybrid vehicle has a more beneficial effect on the environment than the so-called zero-emission battery electric vehicle. This is because the energy for BEVs is normally derived from a fossil-fuel powered generating station, and the overall system efficiency including distribution is low. Even if practical fuel-cell powered electric vehicles can be realised, a hybrid arrangement may still be advantageous for reducing the power unit size, and providing rapid start-up and response.

Later in this chapter, we will examine the impact of land transport on environmental pollution, and discuss the various options for the reduction of emissions. In particular, we will show how hybrid vehicles can make a major contribution.

1.3 Emissions and pollution in the urban environment due to transportation: an historical perspective

The problem of emissions and pollution due to transport is by no means a recent phenomenon. In ancient Roman times, restrictions were placed on the movements of animal-drawn vehicles in order to reduce the levels of noise and traffic congestion in large cities. The polluting effects of large numbers of animals in an urban environment can be quite overpowering. By the nineteenth century, most large European cities were subjected to appalling levels of pollutants resulting from the burning of coal. Overall, only a small proportion of this was attributable to rail transport, but soot deposition turned buildings around major railway stations to a uniform grimy black. Some respite was obtained in the early twentieth century by the introduction of legislation banning the use of open coal fires in inner city areas. However, the notorious London 'smogs' did not disappear until the local coal-fired power stations were removed after the Second World War. London is not naturally foggy, and nowadays fog is quite rare there.

The polluting effects due to the internal combustion engine were less immediately obvious than those of coal firing, but nevertheless, the enormous expansion of traffic during the latter half of the last century has led to high levels of atmospheric pollutants in urban areas, and these were found to be producing significant adverse effect on human health. The high levels of oxides of nitrogen and sulphur even started to have a noticeable impact on the exterior fabric of buildings. Motor vehicles were also responsible for high levels of carbon monoxide, lead compounds, unburned hydrocarbons and particulate matter, all of which represent serious health hazards. Fine particulates smaller than 10 microns in diameter (<PM10) containing volatile organic compounds (VOCs) are increasingly considered to be a major health hazard, and are estimated by Bown [1.1] to be the cause of over 10,000 premature deaths in the UK per year. These fine particulates are known to be carcinogenic.

According to the London Atmospheric Emissions Inventory [1.2], the road transport sector is now the major source of urban air pollution in the United Kingdom. Figure 1.3 shows the contribution by road transport to atmospheric emissions in London and in the UK as a whole in 1990.

Emission	London	UK
NOx	75%	38%
CO	97%	62%
Volatile organic compounds	53%	61%
Particulates	77%	28%
CO_2	29%	22%

Figure 1.3:   The contribution of road transport to atmospheric emissions in London and in the UK as a whole.

As a result of the rapid post-war increase in the number of road vehicles, the level of emissions in the local environment produced a particularly strong effect in the area of the Los Angeles Basin, which is naturally prone to misty conditions. Here the pollutants frequently combined with the mist to form a dense smog. Apart from the aspect of health hazard, the prolonged periods of poor visibility began to have a significant economic impact. As a consequence, legislation to reduce emissions was introduced in Southern California, starting in the 1970s. The Californian lead was followed with varying time lags elsewhere in the world, particularly in Europe.

Following the success of the early moves, Southern California progressively reduced the levels of permitted emissions, and finally attempted to introduce measures that would reduce vehicle emissions to zero by promoting the development of battery electric vehicles. This initiative was, however, hopelessly over-optimistic in terms of the capabilities of the required technologies, and currently more realistically attainable goals are being set. These changes should encourage the development of hybrid vehicles. The subjects of emission regulations, and the Californian zero emissions initiative are dealt with later in this chapter.

1.4 The global climatic problem

Although it was the local urban environment that provided the initial spur for emissions reduction, a growing appreciation of the potentially calamitous effects of so-called 'greenhouse gas' production on the global environment has provided a new impetus. The countries of Northern Europe are particularly susceptible to the effects of global warming, which it is feared may trigger the switching off of the warm water Gulf-stream. If this happens, Northern Europe would become much colder, and a new 'ice age' would develop.

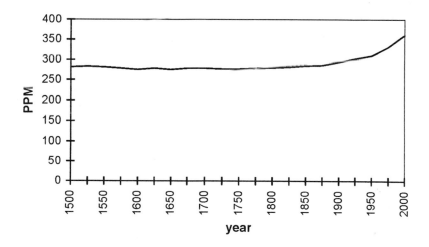

Figure 1.4: The historic trend in atmospheric CO_2 concentrations.

Figure 1.4 shows the historic trend in atmospheric CO_2 concentrations, from Gray [1.3]. The escalation in concentration over the last half century is generally agreed to be the result of human activity. It has been estimated that emissions of greenhouse gases need to be cut back to no more than 60% of the 1990 levels to achieve a halting of the trend in global warming. Carbon dioxide is the gas most closely identified with the greenhouse effect, although methane emissions from various sources including land-fill sites also represent a problem. In recognition of the problem, an agreement to limit man-made emissions was made by some 150 nations at the 1992 Earth Summit in Rio. In 1997, at a follow-up conference in Kyoto, it was agreed that the developed countries should set firm targets to cut carbon dioxide emissions by an average of 5.2% relative to the values in 1990 by the years 2008 to 2012. This was known as the Kyoto protocol. Unfortunately, the political will to fully implement the intentions of Kyoto is lacking in many countries, with the United States in particular being reluctant to face the short-term political and economic problems associated with any move that might raise the cost of energy to industry or the motorist. This is particularly unfortunate, as it is estimated that the United States currently produces about a quarter of the carbon dioxide emissions of the developed world. Canada and Australia also produce large amounts, and are similarly reluctant to commit to the Kyoto agreements.

In 1996, transport accounted for 31% of CO_2 emissions in the USA [1.4] and is rapidly becoming a major source of CO_2 emissions in many parts of the world. In Europe at least, some progress is being made towards a reduction of these emissions. This has primarily taken the form of using taxation to encourage the use of low emission vehicles. In the UK, vehicles are now taxed on a four-band scale that is related to the amount of CO_2 produced per kilometre (g/km), and additional incentives are in place for the use of alternative fuels.

Hybrid propulsion systems provide a method of improving the propulsion efficiency and hence reducing emissions of CO_2. The introduction of the Toyota Prius hybrid car with its low fuel consumption of 62 mpg (4.6 litres/100 km) on an urban driving cycle, has demonstrated that hybrid propulsion is a practical reality. This vehicle has been placed in the lowest vehicle taxation band in the UK.

1.5 Vehicle emissions legislation

Exhaust emissions from vehicles have been subject to regulation since the 1970s, particularly in America, though recently standards throughout Europe and the US are becoming similar. The emissions standards apply to passenger cars, vans and heavy duty vehicles. The European directives concern emissions of carbon monoxide, total hydrocarbons, oxides of nitrogen and, in the case of diesel vehicles, particulate matter.

1.5.1 The Auto-Oil programme

The European vehicle exhaust emissions standards, (EURO I to IV) have been developed within the remit of the European Commission's Auto-Oil 2000 programme. This is the result of collaboration between the automotive industry, the fuel industry and the Commission. These standards have the aim of meeting future air quality objectives, particularly in urban areas, based on the WHO's health and environmental guidelines. The aim is to reduce total overall vehicle emissions by up to 70% in 2010 compared with the 1990 level (Hitchcock *et al.* [1.5]) even allowing for the expected increase in traffic volumes.

1.5.2 Passenger car standards

The first European regulations applied to passenger cars seeking type approval from 1970. Since then, progressively tighter regulations have been introduced. In 1991 the regulations were thoroughly reviewed, and from 1993, they applied to type approval of passenger cars, effectively requiring the introduction of three-way catalytic converters for petrol (gasoline) cars (NSCA [1.6]). Figure 1.5 illustrates the effect of the gradual tightening of the regulations from the introduction of stage 1 (EURO I) limits in 1993 through to the stage 4 limits now agreed for introduction in 2005. In effect the limits require a 50% reduction in passenger car exhaust emissions. Note that the emissions are measured in grams/km, which favours the introduction of smaller fuel-efficient cars. Stages 1 to 3 could easily be met by improvements in engine design and exhaust treatment measures. Stage 4 presents a challenge, but one which the introduction of hybrid propulsion technology could readily meet.

	Date	Emissions in g/km				
		CO	HC	NOx	HC+NOx	PM
EURO I	1993	2.72			0.97	0.14
EURO II	1996	2.2 (1.0)			0.5 (0.7)	(0.08)
EURO III	2000	2.2 (0.64)	0.2	0.15 (0.5)	(0.56)	(0.05)
EURO IV	2005	1.0 (0.5)	0.1	0.08 (0.25)	(0.3)	(0.025)

Figure 1.5:   EU Emissions Legislation for Passenger Cars (after Hitchcock *et al.* [1.5]). Values in brackets are for Diesel-engined vehicles.

1.5.3 California

California has been responsible for the introduction of strict emission reduction requirements for vehicles, and these requirements have gradually been adopted by the rest of the United States and many other nations. Figure 1.6 shows the current emissions limits for passenger cars in California. These limit values are now comparable to those in the EU. For example the Californian Low Emission Vehicle (LEV) standard is similar to EURO III and the Ultra Low Emission Vehicle (ULEV) standard is broadly comparable to EURO IV (Hitchcock *et al.* [1.5]).

	Date	Emissions in g/km				
		CO	HC	NOx	HC+NOx	PM (particulates)
Current	1996	2.11	0.078	0.25	0.328	0.05
LEV		2.11	0.05	0.12	0.17	0.05
ULEV		1.1	0.02	0.12	0.14	0.02
ZEV		0.0	0.0	0.0	0.0	0.0

Figure 1.6:   Californian Emission Limits for Light Duty
Vehicles (after Hitchcock *et al.* [1.5]).

The major difference between the legislation in the European Union and California is that, in the European Union, all new vehicles produced past a certain date must comply with the regulations, whereas in California the regulations apply to a specified and increasing proportion of the vehicles sold by each manufacturer. This allows the emission requirements to be phased in over a period of time. Californian attempts to introduce an increasing proportion of zero emission vehicles (ZEVs) are described in 1.5.6 below.

1.5.4 Van emission standards

Special standards had to be introduced for light vans in Europe because of the range of sizes. Passenger car standards could be applied to the smaller vans but two upper weight classes were introduced to allow proportionally greater emission levels.

1.5.5 Heavy goods vehicles

Legislation for heavier vehicles proved more complicated because of the wide variation in vehicle size. Rather than increase the number of categories, it was decided to limit emissions in terms of grams per kWh rather than grams per km. This could be applied to any engine size. Emission limits for larger vehicles were thus introduced into the EU in 1982 and by 1988 heavy goods vehicle emissions (per vehicle) had reduced by some 30% (Hitchcock *et al.* [1.5]). Since 1990 the legislation has been steadily tightened in a similar pattern to that for passenger cars, as shown in figure 1.7. These limits apply to the engines rather than the vehicles so as to cater for all sizes. Figure 1.7 shows the current and proposed future limits, including the Enhanced Environmentally friendly Vehicle (EEV). As with passenger cars the limits for 2000 were derived from the Auto-Oil programme.

	Date	Emission Limits – g/kWh			
		CO	HC	NOx	PM (particulates)
Pre-EURO I	1990	9.0	1.6	11.5	
EURO I	1993	4.5	1.1	8.0	0.36
EURO II	1996	4.0	1.1	7.0	0.15
EURO III	2001	2.1	0.66	5.0	0.1
EEV	2001	1.5	0.25	2.0	0.02
EURO IV	2005	1.5	0.46	3.5	0.02
EURO V	2008	1.5	0.46	2	0.02

Figure 1.7: EU emission limits for heavy engines (after reference [1.7]).

1.5.6 The Californian zero emissions requirement

Following the success of the initial set of emissions requirements in California, the California Air Resources Board initiated the controversial CARB mandate which required road vehicle manufacturers to build and sell an increasing proportion of zero-emission (ZEV) vehicles to the public. This in practice meant battery electric vehicles (BEVs). Despite the best efforts of the industry and considerable expenditure on development work, however, the American public showed little enthusiasm for these vehicles. Honda stopped making its EV-plus after two years, and in 2000 GM announced that it would cease production of its EV1 due to lack of demand. The advances in battery technology, though significant, were nowhere near sufficient to produce an acceptable vehicle, except for specialist purposes.

A rethink has thus been necessary. One partial loophole in the original requirement was that 60% of the ZEVs could be replaced by cars that earn ZEV credits if they have extended ULEV performance, and more credits if they have an electric range of more than 20 miles. This opens the door to hybrid vehicles, which is encouraging, as the Californian legislators were at first reluctant to consider a role for hybrid vehicles. It was believed that they would inhibit the development of advanced battery technology, which was perceived to be the ideal solution. This resistance has now softened, but attention is being focused on the new Holy Grail of the fuel cell, the merits of which are discussed later.

1.6 Emission reduction and fuel saving measures

Virtually all current road vehicles are propelled by internal combustion engines (diesel and spark ignition) running on carbon-based fuels. Fuel saving on these vehicles has the advantage of reducing all pollutants as well as CO_2 emissions. Improvements in fuel efficiency could contribute significantly to a reduction in both greenhouse emission and atmospheric pollution. Emissions due to road traffic are closely related to the energy consumption.

The problem of reducing emissions may be tackled in three basic ways:

1.   by changes to the transportation infrastructure
2.   by improvements to current vehicle technologies
3.   by the introduction of new technologies

1.6.1 Changes to transportation infrastructure

Changes to the infrastructure clearly have the potential for significant benefits, but they are hostages to political will. If we assess the benefit per person rather than per vehicle, then the impetus for development could point towards larger urban fleet vehicles rather than private cars. Figure 1.8 shows the present energy consumption per passenger km for a range of vehicle types. This suggests that for maximum benefit, short-term development should be concentrated on the hybrid bus.

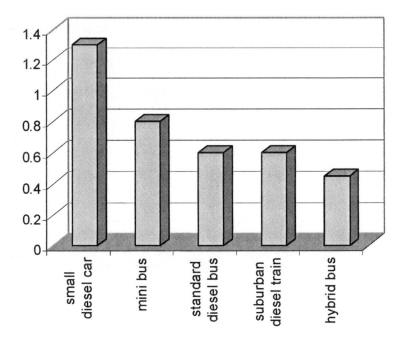

Figure 1.8:   Energy consumption by mode (MJ per passenger km).

There are unfortunately significant political problems in trying to persuade the travelling public to leave their cars at home or in a 'park and ride' car park, and make use of public transport. A major shift to public transport can only occur if a convenient and reliable service is provided, and this requires a high level of capital investment and long-term planning. In particular, government expenditure is required, as the time-scale and the return on investment of purely private capital is rarely attractive to investors. Many of the countries of Europe and Scandinavia have been active in trying to provide effective public transport systems and cycleways in urban areas. In the UK and the US, efforts have been generally weaker.

Outside urban areas, the advantages of point to point movement are likely to ensure that the car will remain the most popular form of transport for medium distance travel. About the only system change that can be invoked is the reduction of speed limits. As described in Chapter 5, the power required to overcome aerodynamic resistance is proportional to the vehicle speed to the third power (V^3), and at 70 mph, (112 km/h), a 10% reduction in traffic speeds would lead to a 23% reduction of engine power requirement on a domestic car. Speed reductions of this order would therefore reduce fuel consumption and CO_2 emissions considerably. However, these advantages have to be weighed against the increase in journey times and the economic effects of the slower movement of goods and people. At present there appears to be little political will to reduce speed limits on motorways. In the US, freeway speed limits are already much lower than those in Europe, and in view of the large distances covered by motor vehicles there, further scope for speed restrictions seems limited.

1.7 Improvements to current vehicle technologies

Throughout the World there is strong popular demand for increasing use of private motor cars. Many national governments have attempted to counter this by investing in improved public transport infrastructure, but their success in stemming the tide of car growth has so far been only partially successful. The development of current emission reduction technologies has, however, generally benefited from the actions of governments. Perhaps the most obvious example was the requirement in most developed countries for vehicles to meet stringent emission targets, a move that led to the removal of lead additives, and the fitting of catalytic converters to petrol-engined (gasoline-engined) vehicles.

1.7.1 Catalytic converters

Catalytic converters act on exhaust emissions to reduce the levels of CO, HC and NOx. They are not very effective in reducing particulate emissions, and they are also ineffective when cold, which is the case on a substantial proportion of urban journeys. It has been found that 70 to 85% of CO emissions occur during the warm-up period from a cold start. According to Whitelegg [1.8], catalytic converters can reduce NOx emissions due to road transport by up to 40%, with even greater effects on the levels of hydrocarbon and CO emissions once the catalysts reach running temperature. SOx emissions have been reduced by lowering the sulphur content of the fuels, a move that has been encouraged in the UK by the reduction of tax on low-sulphur fuels.

The fitting of catalytic converters was aimed at improving the air quality in urban environments, but had the unfortunate side effect of reducing the fuel efficiency and consequently increasing fuel consumption (and hence CO_2 production). The reduction in power resulting from the fitting of catalytic converters led to an overall increase in the size of engines being installed. The measure has also resulted in a major increase in the use of the rare metal platinum.

1.7.2 Changing to diesel engines

One way to reduce the fuel consumption of road vehicles, and consequently lower the production of CO_2 is to move away from the petrol (gasoline) engine, to the significantly more efficient diesel engine. Carbon monoxide emissions are also much lower in the diesel engine, and the fitting of catalytic converters is not yet considered necessary. Diesel engines are notorious for the high levels of fine particulates that are produced, and these have been shown to be a major health hazard. However, as a result of the high level of interest, there have recently been major technical developments. Particulate emissions have been significantly reduced, and various further strategies are under development. These include particulate traps, catalytic conversion, and the use of ionisation of either the input air, or the exhaust gases [1.9].

In Europe, diesel engines are used for virtually all heavy goods vehicles and buses, but in California, regulations governing particulate emissions have led to the use of the less-efficient petrol engines for buses. Thus, as with the catalytic converter, legislation aimed at reducing local emission levels has had a negative impact on the global greenhouse gas problem.

In the UK, the scales of charges for vehicle duty were originally intended to be related only to the amount of carbon dioxide produced per 100 km. This would, however, have strongly favoured the diesel, and thereby increased the production of particulates. In the final version, therefore, the duty for diesel-engined vehicles has been factored up to discourage any strong early move towards diesel power.

If the problem of diesel particulates can be overcome, a more widespread adoption of the diesel engine will almost certainly follow. Industry sources predict that about half the private cars sold in Europe will be diesel powered by the year 2005 when the EURO IV emission limits take effect.

1.7.3 Improvements in engine efficiency

Despite over a century of steady development, the efficiency of the internal combustion engine has been increased dramatically in recent years. Technical advances have included the introduction of direct fuel injection to both diesel and petrol engines, with electronic control, and the use of variable valve timing and valve lift. Further development is still possible, but there is an upper theoretical limit to the efficiency of these engines, and eventually, if significantly higher propulsive efficiency is required, other forms of propulsion system will be required.

1.7.4 Reducing vehicle power requirements

In order to develop strategies for improving fuel efficiency, account has to be taken of how energy is dissipated. Figure 1.9 shows the proportions in which the engine output energy is dissipated for a typical car in urban traffic, as given by Hughes [1.10]. The remainder of the total energy originally available in the fuel is mainly accounted for by losses in the engine, which are assumed to be proportional to the output energy.

	Energy as a proportion of the total energy supplied by the fuel	Energy as a proportion of the total energy transmitted to the wheels
Aerodynamic Drag	4%	22%
Rolling Resistance	6%	33%
Braking	8%	45%
Total	**18%**	**100%**

Figure 1.9: Distribution of energy dissipation in a typical car in urban use.

1.7.5 Reducing aerodynamic drag

As indicated in Figure 1.9, in urban driving, aerodynamic drag represents an important contribution to the energy used. At steady cruising speeds of around 120 km/h, aerodynamic drag becomes the dominant factor, and about 75% of the final output power of a domestic car is attributable to aerodynamic drag. The remainder of the power is used to overcome the rolling resistance. Thus, a 10% improvement in the aerodynamic efficiency, corresponding to a 10% reduction in the drag coefficient (defined in Chapter 5) will produce a 7.5% reduction in fuel consumption. In practice, the results of improved aerodynamic design have caused average drag coefficients to fall from a value of around 0.45 in the 1970s to around 0.3 today, and this factor alone should have improved fuel consumption in cruise by around 23%. Further savings of around 10% are still possible with improved aerodynamic design, particularly in respect of the underbody. Significant improvements in the fuel consumption of large commercial vehicles can also be obtained, although tyre rolling resistance tends to represent a greater proportion of the total. Even at urban traffic speeds of 25 mph, a 10% reduction in aerodynamic drag would reduce the power requirement of a typical car by about 2%. At this same speed, the streamlining of buses can result in a fuel consumption reduction of around 2% relative to that produced by the traditional brick-shaped vehicles.

About half the improvement in vehicle fuel economy that has been realised in the last two or three decades can be attributed to improved aerodynamic design. The significance of vehicle aerodynamics is dealt with in more detail in Chapter 5. All aspects of road vehicle aerodynamic design are covered by Barnard [1.11].

1.7.6 The advantages of vehicle weight reduction

Reductions in vehicle weight would result in a lower rolling resistance and a reduced energy requirement for acceleration: the latter factor being the more significant. The use of aluminium in car bodies has been pioneered notably by Audi, and the adoption of this material is likely to become more common in future. For cars, overall weight reductions of between 5 and 10% seem feasible [1.12] but the scope for further reduction is limited. Unfortunately, at present, customer preferences and the requirements of safety are pushing up the weight of cars, and there is no sign that this trend is likely to be reversed in the near future. For heavy goods vehicles, the potential for weight savings is rather lower, as it is the load rather than the vehicle weight that is the primary factor.

The rolling resistance of tyres has been the subject of a great deal of research. Unfortunately, although reductions in tyre rolling resistance have been demonstrated, it has proved difficult to achieve major reductions without compromising the braking and cornering abilities. The rolling resistance of steel wheels on a track is only about 4% of that for rubber tyres on a road, which gives rail vehicles an inherent advantage over road transport in terms of potential energy efficiency.

1.7.7 The use of alternative fuels

Compressed natural gas (CNG). CNG, which is mainly methane, is potentially a low cost, low emission fuel, and is already in use in commercial vehicle fleets. CNG used in place of existing fuels would produce a significant improvement in urban air quality. Poulton [1.12] gives the possible reduction in emissions due to conversion to CNG in urban transport as up to 33%. However, the effect on global warming could be offset by the corresponding increase in methane emissions, which have a much higher 'greenhouse' effect than CO_2.

Liquefied petroleum gas (LPG). LPG, which is mainly propane, is also used in fleet operations, with similar benefits. LPG has the advantage over CNG of simpler distribution and refuelling facilities, and is becoming more widely available to private car users.

Alcohols. Methanol and ethanol are also readily suitable for use in internal combustion engines. They contain a relatively high proportion of hydrogen, which burns to produce water, and the emissions of CO_2 are therefore lower than for oil-based fuels. Alcohols can be produced readily from the fermentation and distillation of organic waste. Carbon dioxide is produced in this process, but while the plants are growing, they absorb carbon dioxide and release oxygen, so the whole process of production and use can be considered to represent a close loop, with no net increase in CO_2. The final distillation process does however require the use of energy.

Alcohol has been in use in a number of countries as a gasoline additive. In Brazil, ethanol has been added to gasoline at 22% for some 15 years, and there are plans to add vegetable oil to diesel fuel. However, there are concerns about the levels of toxic organic compounds, such as formaldehyde, that are produced by alcohol, and further work on emission reduction is necessary in this area. There are also safety concerns over the use of alcohol fuels, as the flame is almost invisible, and accidental ignition can go unnoticed for some time. The possible ecological and economic impact of a large-scale move to alcohol fuels would also need to be carefully considered.

Several other synthetic fuels are under development. These are designed to produce low proportions of harmful and greenhouse gases. Arguably, the most promising alternative fuel is hydrogen, and this is dealt with under the discussions of new technologies below.

1.7.8 Limits to the effectiveness of improvements to existing technology

Car manufacturers are responding effectively to emission reduction requirements by using the above developments to produce cleaner, more efficient, engines. Combining all these measures could probably enable the CO_2 emission target to be met if it were not for the anticipated world-wide growth in the number of vehicles. The number of cars on the road in the year 2000 was estimated to be roughly 700 million, but this is estimated to grow to over 2000 million by 2050. Meeting global carbon dioxide reduction targets set for that year would thus require a three to four fold reduction in fuel consumption per vehicle. It is evident therefore that in the longer term, more radical solutions will need to be developed.

1.8 New technologies

1.8.1 Electric vehicles

As stated earlier, the initial impetus for the reduction emissions came from the problem of urban air quality. This has spurred on the development of the electric car, which is emission free at the point of use. However, this has not yet led to any significant market for such vehicles, because of their higher initial cost, short range and longer 'refuelling' time compared with the conventional car. The

Californian attempt to create an artificial market has already been described above. Despite considerable efforts by manufacturers and the setting up of a pilot system of electrical recharging stations, the number of electric vehicles actually sold was insignificant, and the ambitious plans were repeatedly scaled back. Similarly, Japan planned for the introduction of 20,000 BEVs by the year 2000, but the number actually sold by that date was negligible.

The reasons for the lack of consumer enthusiasm are fairly obvious. BEVs so far constructed have been of the order of 300 to 1000 kg heavier than corresponding conventional vehicles, and between 50 to 100% more expensive. Experimental vehicles have shown ranges of up to 70 miles or more under favourable conditions with unconventional batteries, but at low ambient temperatures, and with a battery that is not new, the practical range can drop to as little as half this amount. It was at one time hoped that the development of advanced batteries would make the BEV a more practical vehicle, but as described in Chapter 3, this promise has not been fully realised. The new batteries, though superior in most respects to the older lead/acid type, still show practical weaknesses such as a poor ability to hold charge or a poor cycle life at high currents. Progress to date has not been sufficient to improve the attractiveness of BEVs for general purpose transport.

There does appear to be a limited market for BEVs in some special cases. These include inner city short route buses, and short range fleet delivery vehicles. Electric milk delivery vehicles are still widely used in the UK, and have been, since they replaced the horse and cart in the early post-war years. Silent operation in the early hours of the morning, a short and consistent route, and the fact that no energy is consumed during the high proportion of the time that the vehicle is stationary, give the BEV an advantage for this application.

Apart from the lack of customer appeal, there has been a growing appreciation of the fact that although BEVs may improve the local environment in urban areas, they will actually serve to increase the overall emissions of CO_2 if the primary electricity is generated from fossil fuel sources. This is due to the very low overall 'well to wheel' efficiency of the total system. Starting with the power station, electricity is normally generated by a steam plant or gas turbines, which have an efficiency of between 20 to 30%. To this must be added transmission and transformer efficiency, which may be around 95%. Losses incurred during the charging and discharging of the battery typically result in an efficiency of 75%. The efficiency of the motor and final transmission may be as high as 90%. The overall efficiency is thus of the order of 15%, which compares unfavourably with the 35% or so that is theoretically obtainable with an internal combustion engine and mechanical transmission in a high efficiency hybrid configuration.

From this it will be seen that, in term of global emissions, BEVs will actually make the situation worse, unless the electricity is generated from non fossil-fuel sources. One example of a case where electrical propulsion coupled to non fossil-fuel sources has been implemented is in La Rochelle in Western France, where there has been a pioneering introduction of a central urban zone in which only electric vehicles are permitted. Because of the high proportion of nuclear power generation in France, the scheme at La Rochelle can be said to qualify as producing a reduction in both local and global emissions. The long-term problems of nuclear power are, however, well understood, and it is only short-term political factors that favour any expansion in capacity.

If environmental considerations are given full weight, then any large-scale introduction of BEVs will have to await a significant move towards the generation of electricity from safe, renewable sources such as wind, wave and solar energy. In view of the problems associated with BEVs, enthusiasm for this form of propulsion is now waning, with attention being directed instead towards fuel cells, as described below.

1.8.2 The use of hydrogen as a fuel

Hydrogen represents almost the ideal fuel at the end-user stage, since its primary emission product is water vapour. Some caution is required however, because large amounts of water vapour can produce an unpleasantly hot, humid and misty environment in urban areas, and can contribute to the greenhouse effect. Hydrogen can be used as a fuel in modified internal combustion engines, but as it is burned with air, the high temperatures involved result in the formation of a certain amount of undesirable NOx. Gas turbines can be run on hydrogen, and indeed gaseous hydrogen was used for the first run of the first successful gas turbine (built by von Ohain in Germany in 1937). In gas turbines, the peak temperatures are lower than in reciprocating engines, and NOx emissions are much reduced. Currently, gas turbines are not generally considered to be suitable for automotive applications, but they may nevertheless reappear in larger hybrid vehicles for reasons that are discussed in Chapter 4.

The most efficient prime mover for use with hydrogen appears to be the fuel cell. Fuel cells combine hydrogen with atmospheric oxygen to produce water and electricity. The conversion process is highly efficient at up to 70%, which compares favourably with the overall efficiency of petrol and diesel engines that is in the range of 30% to 40% maximum.

Because fuel cells can operate at relatively low temperatures, the product of the hydrogen/oxygen reaction is almost nothing but water vapour. Fuel cell powered vehicles, such as the Necar and Nebus from Daimler-Chrysler have already been demonstrated, and most of the major motor manufacturers are supporting research and development programmes. Figure 1.10 shows the Ford Prodigy fuel cell concept car, which was shown at the Birmingham Motor Show in 2000. The technical merits and limitations of the fuel cell are discussed in some depth in Chapter 4.

The adoption of hydrogen as a fuel for road vehicles presents a number of major problems. Firstly onboard storage is not easy. If stored as a gas, the pressure has to be very high to avoid excessive volume, and if stored as a cryogenic liquid, the temperature has to be maintained at the extremely low temperature of $-253°C$.

Figure 1.10:   The Ford Prodigy fuel cell concept car shown at the Birmingham
                Motor Show in 2000.

Another option is to store the hydrogen in the form of hydrides, or in carbon nano-tube fibres, but both these options tend to be very bulky. The hydrogen may alternatively be reformed on board from gasoline or hydrogen-rich liquid fuels such as methanol, as discussed in Chapter 4. Again, this is a bulky solution, and results in some problematic by-products.

The main problem with the use of hydrogen is that it is not a primary fuel. It has to be produced, and a large amount of energy is consumed in its production. If this energy is derived from carbon-based fuels, the net environmental impact will be detrimental, since it is unlikely that the overall 'well-to-wheel' efficiency will be as high as using such fuels directly in an internal combustion engine. Put simply, if the hydrogen is produced using energy from fossil fuel sources, more CO_2 will be produced than if the fossil fuel were used directly in an i.c. engine. Reforming from ethanol is another option, but the ethanol also requires a large amount of energy in the distillation part of its production.

Electrolysis of water using electricity generated from nuclear power would be an option that would not involve the production of carbon dioxide, but the use of nuclear power raises its own set of major environmental problems. The ideal long-term solution would appear to lie in the production of hydrogen using electricity from renewable sources such as wind, waves, hydro and solar energy. Generating hydrogen by these methods also overcomes the problem of matching the power requirement to the unsteady natural supply. There is at last some evidence that the generation of electricity by renewable sources is being taken seriously by national governments, and its use for the production of hydrogen seems the most promising way forward. This is however a long-term solution. Apart from the time involved in planning and constructing the new generating plants, it will be necessary to set up comprehensive hydrogen supply systems, which will require a very large capital investment.

A further problem with the use of hydrogen is that unless it is reformed on board, it has to be stored either cryogenically at −253°C or compressed to a very high pressure (anything up to 340 atmospheres is being considered). Both options require the expenditure of a large amount of energy, with attendant CO_2 production, unless a renewable source is used.

If hydrogen fuelling is introduced, then it is likely that the technology will initially be used for fleet transport vehicles. Fleet transport, road and rail, presently accounts for about 34% of CO_2 emissions due to land transport in the UK (Hughes [1.10]) and hence around 8% of overall CO_2 emissions. Due to their high efficiency, fuel cell powered vehicles will require a significantly smaller volume of gas than would be needed for reciprocating engines, and this will have a beneficial influence on the problems of storage and transportation of the hydrogen.

Hydrogen fuelling will not decrease the need for hybrid propulsion systems. The rapid response to power demand provided by stored energy devices, and their ability to absorb braking loads will still be an advantage. Also, as with i.c. engined hybrids, by using the stored energy to meet the short-term peak power demands, the size and weight of the fuel cell can be reduced, and it may be run at a more constant loading.

1.9 So why hybrid? The case for hybrid vehicle technology

The hybrid propulsion concept is a complement rather than an alternative to the various options for reducing emissions and fuel consumption outlined above. It provides a means of improving the efficiency of almost any vehicle propulsion system. The three main advantages of a hybrid system are:

1. Energy normally lost in braking can be recovered and stored for later use.
2. The size of the primary engine power source can be reduced.
3. The primary power source operates at a more constant load, which benefits the optimisation process and leads to higher efficiency.

Hybrid propulsion systems can produce additional benefits depending on the type of prime mover used.

4. For petrol and diesel-engined vehicles, the motor can be switched off for short intervals when the vehicle is stationary.
5. For gas turbine powered vehicles, the slow response rate to changes in power demand can be overcome by use of boosts from stored energy.

6. For external combustion engines such as the steam engine or the Stirling engine, the stored energy system can be used while the combustion process is warming up.
7. For fuel cell-powered vehicles, the hybrid system can also overcome the initial warm up problem and can meet rapid power demand changes.

1.9.1 The advantages of brake energy recovery

The energy used for acceleration results in an increase in kinetic energy of the vehicle. In conventional vehicles, this energy is dissipated as heat in the brakes during deceleration. In urban driving, considerable use is made of the brakes, with the vehicle frequently being brought to rest. It has been variously estimated (e.g. Hughes [1.10]) that brake energy accounts for around 40% to 45% of the typical energy consumption of a car in an urban cycle (see figure 1.9), so the potential for energy savings and reduced CO_2 emissions is considerable.

Conventional vehicles are not provided with any means of recovering any of this brake energy, but one of the main advantages of hybrid vehicle propulsion is its inherent potential for such recovery. The advantages can only be realised, however, if the system is suitably optimised. Hybrid vehicles tend to be heavier than their conventional counterparts, and often contain several stages of energy conversion. The conversion efficiencies of the various components, and the optimisation of their integration, therefore represent critically important aspects of hybrid vehicle design. These are discussed in detail in later chapters.

Battery electric vehicles also allow a certain amount of brake energy recovery, but this is limited by the generally low storage efficiency of batteries. Typically, less than 75% of the energy input to a battery can be extracted from it; the remainder is lost in heat. After allowance is made for the conversion efficiencies of the various components in the transmission system, the resulting overall amount of brake energy that is recovered in a battery electric vehicle seldom exceeds 40%. As will be shown in Chapter 3, batteries are not the ideal energy storage device for hybrid vehicles.

1.9.2 Advantages of hybrid vehicles in urban driving

The advantages of hybrid propulsion are mostly felt in urban driving where regenerative braking, reduced primary engine size and engine switch-off can produce major energy savings. In high-speed cruise, the hybrid gains only from the effect of the smaller primary motor working at a higher, more efficient loading. This is borne out by the Prius, which returns a commendable fuel consumption of around 4.6 litres/100 km (62 mpg) on the urban driving cycle, but a more modest 5 litres/100 km (55.4 mpg) on the extra-urban cycle.

In most developed countries, the majority of domestic car journeys are in urban areas. According to Papacostas [1.13], 75% of journeys made in the US are in urban areas. Hughes [1.10] also gives the proportion of car traffic in urban areas (km per capita per week) as 75%. As shown in figure 1.11, it can then be deduced

	Percentage reduction	Reference
CO_2 emissions due to land transport in USA.	31%	[1.1]
Journeys made in urban areas in USA.	75%	[1.13]
Energy normally lost in braking in urban driving.	40%-45%	[1.10]
Energy potentially recoverable by regenerative braking.	50%-80%	
Overall potential for fuel savings and CO_2 reduction.	4.7%- 8%	

Figure 1.11:   Potential for the reduction in CO_2 emissions in the USA by use of regenerative braking.

that the use of brake energy recovery could produce a reduction of 8% in CO_2 emissions in the USA. A similar figure might reasonably be expected for other developed countries.

Apart from energy savings, the improved efficiency of the hybrid vehicle in urban areas means that the noxious emissions are reduced, and local pollution concentrations are lowered. A further benefit is the reduced engine noise level. The Prius, for example, starts without the usual engine cranking noise, and moves off silently using its electric motor. In hybrid buses, it is normal to use an electric transmission system, which produces a smooth acceleration uninterrupted by gear changes.

1.10 References

[1.1] Bown, W., Dying from too much dust, *New Scientist*, March 12, pp. 12-13, 1994.
[1.2] Hutchinson, D., Buckingham, C., Clewley, L., Shah, S. and Sadler, L., *London Atmospheric Emissions Inventory*, London Research Centre, London, 1997.
[1.3] Gray, V. R., Atmospheric Carbon Dioxide, *Greenhouse Bulletin*, No. 120, Feb. 1999.
[1.4] US Energy Information Administration, *Emissions Greenhouse Gases in the United States 1996*, URL:http://www.eia.doe.gov/oiaf/1605/gg97rpt/chap2.html
[1.5] Hitchcock, G., Parker, T., Longhurst, J. W. S. and Simmons, A., Reducing the environmental impact of vehicles in urban areas. Low emission zone concepts: objectives and criteria, *Report D1 for the Nat. Society for Clean Air and Environmental Protection*, Transport and Travel Research, Bristol, 1999.

[1.6]   Pollution Handbook, *National Society for Clean Air and Environmental Protection*, NSCA, Brighton, 1998.

[1.7]   Emission Standards: European Union, *Heavy-Duty Diesel Truck and Bus Engines*, Ecopoint Inc, 1999, www.dieselnet.com/standards/eu/hd.html

[1.8]   Whitelegg, J., *Transport for a Sustainable Future*, Belhaven, London and New York, pp. 50-53, 1993.

[1.9]   Crosse, Jesse, Plasma exhaust promises cleaner diesel, *FT Automotive World, Financial Times Business Ltd.*, September 1999, p. 6.

[1.10] Hughes, P., *Personal Transport and the Greenhouse Effect*, Earthscan, London, pp. 20-29, 1993.

[1.11] Barnard, R. H., *Road Vehicle Aerodynamic Design: 2nd Ed.*, MechAero Publications, St Albans, UK, 2001.

[1.12] Poulton, M. L., *Fuel Efficient Car Technology*, Computational Mechanics Publications, Southampton, p. 53, 1997.

[1.13] Papacostas, C. S. and Prevedouros, P. D., *Transport Engineering and Planning*, Prentice Hall, Englewood Cliffs, p. 257, 1993.

Chapter 2

HYBRID PROPULSION CONFIGURATIONS

2.1 Configuration of hybrid power trains

One of the early attractions of the hybrid vehicle propulsion system was that they would allow operation in pure electric mode in town centres where zero emissions were called for. Out of town, a small i.c. engine could then replenish the charge, and hence extend the range. Vehicles of this type do exist, but the hybrid vehicle concept is now seen more generally as a means of reducing both emissions and fuel consumption. Hybrid propulsion systems achieve this by allowing the use of a small engine operating at high efficiency, and by using energy storage to recover brake energy. Many, but not all hybrid vehicles employ stepless electric transmission systems. To be effective, the hybrid system requires harmonised operation of the engine and energy storage systems in a carefully controlled and optimised manner.

There are two basic types of hybrid drive chain, namely: series and parallel. In the series arrangement illustrated in simple form in figure 2.1, power is drawn from the energy storage, which is continuously charged by the engine. This normally requires electric transmission between the engine and vehicle drive, and thus draws largely on the electric vehicle concept. In this arrangement, the energy storage is usually a battery, but it can take other forms including electromechanical, hydraulic or pneumatic devices. In any case, power conversion is required at each interface, and there is no direct mechanical coupling between the engine and the vehicle drive.

Figure 2.1: Series hybrid arrangement.

In the parallel arrangement shown in figure 2.2, a conventional mechanical transmission between the engine and vehicle wheels is preserved, thus retaining its inherent transmission efficiency. Stored energy is used to supplement the engine power (or to recover brake energy) via a connection to the transmission system.

A second power unit (e.g. a battery and electric motor/generator) is connected mechanically at some point in the drive train. Both these arrangements allow a relatively small prime-mover engine to run mainly at optimum load, with additional power for acceleration being drawn from the battery, which is recharged during deceleration by reversing the power flow.

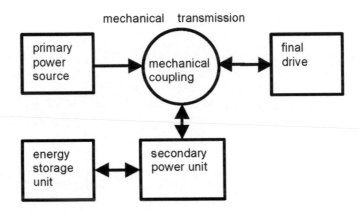

Figure 2.2: Parallel hybrid arrangement.

In an alternative version, shown in figure 2.3, the secondary stored energy power system may be coupled to a separate drive, giving independent front and rear wheel drives.

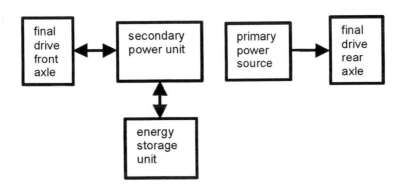

Figure 2.3: An alternative parallel arrangement using four-wheel drive.

This split arrangement was demonstrated by Daimler-Chrysler on a four-wheel drive version of the Dodge Durango, as described by Jesse Crosse [2.1]. The engine of this normally rear-wheel drive sports utility vehicle was downsized from a 5.9 litre V8 to a 3.9 litre V6. A 66 kW Siemens induction motor was installed to drive the front wheels. The electric motor and petrol engine were integrated electronically, and the arrangement allowed regenerative braking. Fuel consumption improved from 15 litres/100 km to 12 litres/100 km: a 20% improvement. This represents an ingenious method of producing both a hybrid and a four-wheel drive without the complexity associated with a mechanical four-wheel drive powertrain.

The advantage of the parallel arrangement is that most of the features of the conventional mechanical transmission system may be retained, thus leading to cost savings and high transmission efficiency. Numerous variants of these configurations are possible, and many have been tried at some stage. Some examples are described later in this chapter.

The labelling of the two types of hybrids as series and parallel can be misleading, particularly as it is possible to have a combination of both methods. For present purposes, we will use the term parallel hybrid to describe vehicles that retain a direct mechanical transmission between the primary motor and the wheels.

2.2 The basic components of a hybrid system

Whether series or parallel, it is convenient to regard the hybrid vehicle and its propulsion system as comprising four components:

1. a prime mover
2. an energy storage facility
3. a transmission system
4. a control system

2.2.1 The prime mover

The prime mover is the main energy source for the vehicle. Examples of hybrid vehicle prime movers include:

- a reciprocating internal combustion engine (diesel or spark ignition)
- a gas turbine
- an external combustion engine (such as a steam engine)
- a fuel cell
- mains electricity supply (as in a hybrid trolleybus or train)
- a battery

The first four must include fuel tanks. A hybrid trolleybus or train enables the vehicle to make use of regenerative braking to reduce the maximum supply current requirement. The choice of a hybrid vehicle based on a battery as a prime mover may seem a little surprising, but by using a high specific-power storage device such as a flywheel or ultracapacitor to provide short bursts of energy, the cycle demands on the main battery may be reduced, and its lifetime consequently extended. Many types of prime mover are potentially suitable for hybrid applications, and some of the more likely contenders are described in greater detail in Chapter 4.

2.2.2 The energy storage facility

This is a relatively short-term source of energy, normally replenished by the prime mover. It serves to assist the prime mover during vehicle acceleration, and ideally, to recover brake energy during deceleration. In addition, if a reciprocating internal combustion engine is used as the main power source, it is also possible to use the stored energy and its power output device to restart the reciprocating engine rapidly and smoothly. It is thus practical to switch the engine off when the vehicle is temporarily stationary.

Forms of energy storage suitable for hybrid vehicles are discussed in further detail in Chapter 3, but examples include:

- batteries
- flywheels
- hydraulic accumulators
- ultracapacitors

2.3 Series hybrid arrangements

A simple example of the series configuration is a battery electric vehicle with an on-board battery charger in the form of an engine-generator set. This arrangement is shown in figure 2.4. The energy storage consists of battery cells that can be charged continuously or intermittently by the engine-generator set. In this arrangement, power can flow either way between the battery and the drive motor, so that during braking, the motor can act as a generator, feeding brake energy back into the battery. The problem with this is that in order to be able to absorb the large amounts of power involved, whilst avoiding rapid deterioration of the batteries, the capacity of the battery storage has to be at least ten times that required simply for energy storage. A further problem is that because of the need for two stages of power conversion, such arrangements have not until recently been regarded as energy efficient. The arrangement does, however, provide a smooth stepless flexible transmission.

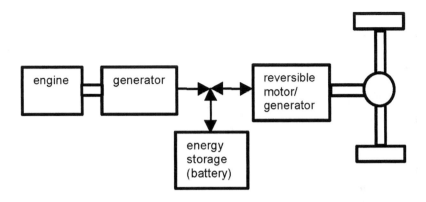

Figure 2.4: Schematic of engine/ battery-electric series hybrid system.

Series hybrid electric vehicles were developed in the 1970s as electric vehicles with on-board engine-generator sets to provide the added range. These sets could be sized either to provide sufficient power to meet the overall average demand, or alternatively, to maintain battery charge during a specified operational time. In both cases, battery power would be used to provide most of the boost power for acceleration.

The series electric hybrid configuration enables a flexible approach to the design of the vehicle by virtue of the fact that it involves electrical, rather than mechanical, transmission between elements. One advantage is the fact that the engine can be located in a soundproof containment at any convenient point on the vehicle. It also becomes easy to provide a very low floor arrangement over the full length of the vehicle, which is particularly attractive for public transport vehicles, and the series hybrid configuration has been widely used in the first generation of hybrid buses.

The electrical arrangement for the series hybrid configuration is shown in figure 2.5. All transmission is electrical, via the DC link. This normally requires a power converter for each element of the system, in order to control the power flow in the form of direct current (DC) from element to element. It may be seen in figures 2.4 and 2.5, that the power flow between the vehicle drive motors and the energy storage is reversible. This is in order to allow regenerative braking, which requires a sink for the regenerated power. If brake energy is to be recovered, then the energy storage unit must be able to accept the regenerated power, and the power flow must be controllable, as this governs the deceleration rate.

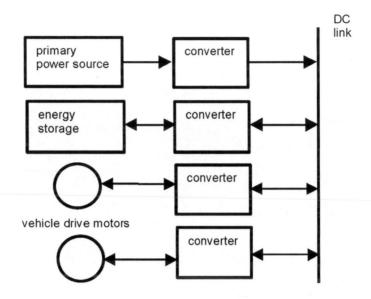

Figure 2.5: Electrical arrangement for the series hybrid configuration.

In current developments using batteries as energy storage, only a limited proportion of the brake energy can be absorbed by the batteries, because of their poor power acceptance capability: i.e. their poor ability to recharge at high power. This problem can be addressed in two ways:

1. by carrying a proportionally higher volume of batteries
2. by use of alternative energy storage systems.

The first approach carries the penalty of increased weight, and considerable development is now underway of more efficient forms of energy storage, as described in the next chapter. Flywheels and ultracapacitors are showing considerable promise in this respect. Several series configuration hybrid vehicles are described in Chapter 7.

2.3.1 Series flywheel-electric arrangements

In a series hybrid electric vehicle, the battery may be either replaced by, or supplemented with, a flywheel system consisting of a flywheel and an associated electrical machine which can be run either as a generator or as a motor. The efficiency of energy storage and release is higher for a flywheel than for a battery, and perhaps more importantly, flywheel systems are better suited than batteries to absorbing the high power levels associated with regenerative braking. The problems of poor cycle life are also avoided. Considerable experience in the operation of such vehicles has now been gained with the CCM and Magnet Motor buses described in Chapter 7. These vehicles incorporate a series arrangement of an i.c. engine and a flywheel. In addition to improved fuel efficiency and lower emissions, these vehicles show a number of advantages over conventional buses, such as lower noise, and smooth stepless transmission.

2.3.2 Flywheel systems with external power supply

An interesting option for a zero emissions passenger transit vehicle is to combine a flywheel storage system with an external electricity supply obtained either by way of a continuous overhead conductor wire, as on a trolleybus, or by temporary connection to a supply while at a stop. In the latter case, the purpose of the flywheel is to store sufficient energy to propel the vehicle between stops. The flywheel is also partially recharged when slowing down, by recovering brake energy. The arrangement is shown schematically in figure 2.6.

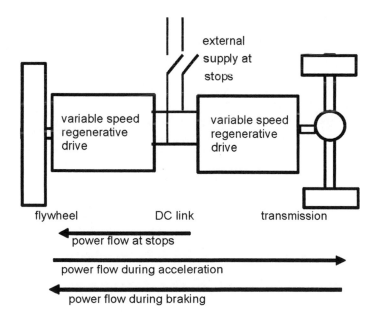

Figure 2.6:   Flywheel propulsion with intermittent external electric power supply, electric transmission and regenerative braking.

An early example of the use of this method was on the Oerlikon Gyrobus, which is described in Chapter 7. This approach was also adopted on a number of small rail vehicles developed by Parry People Movers of Cradley Heath, West Midlands, UK. One example used in an amusement park is shown in figure 2.7. The flywheel was charged by an electric motor connected to an external low voltage DC supply at each stop. A larger vehicle using the same arrangement went into service in Bristol, UK, conveying visitors along the harbourside. This vehicle is also illustrated and described in more detail in Chapter 7. The advantage of this hybrid system compared to a conventional tram or trolleybus is that it obviates the need for the unsightly overhead wires and supports, which are a source of high installation and maintenance costs.

Figure 2.7:   An early Parry flywheel/CVT small rail vehicle (PPM5).

In the alternative approach of continuous connection to external supply by overhead wires, the flywheel serves to reduce the peak demand on the supply system, thereby allowing a greater vehicle capacity on the line. The use of regenerative braking reduces the overall energy demand. This arrangement was tested experimentally on a New York subway train in the 1970s, but the flywheel technology available at the time did not yield sufficient energy savings to warrant its adoption. Flywheel technology has made considerable advances since then, and a similar arrangement has since been adopted in the city of Basel, to increase the capacity of a trolleybus line. The vehicle is shown in figure 2.8. It incorporates a Magnet Motor flywheel unit. As described in Chapter 7, it has shown savings of more than 25% compared to conventional trolleybuses.

Figure 2.8:   The Basel hybrid trolleybus with Magnet Motor flywheel storage system. (Photo courtesy of Magnet Motor GmbH).

2.3.3 Hybrid vehicles with continuously variable mechanical transmission (CVT)

Mechanical CVTs (continuously variable transmissions) are now sufficiently well developed to be used in place of fixed ratio gearboxes in automotive applications. They provide a continuously variable ratio of input to output speed, and thus allow the engine speed to be truly independent of vehicle speed.

The first really successful application of a CVT was in the small Dutch DAF car, which used a belt drive with a pair of drive pulleys with effectively variable diameter. A development of the same system using a metal link belt has been available for some time on the Ford Fiesta. This arrangement produces a smooth, continuously variable automatic transmission.

An early example of a hybrid vehicle employing a CVT was the Gould postal van described by Collie [2.2]. This vehicle used a parallel hybrid configuration with an i.c. engine as the primary power source, and a battery for energy storage. Fuel efficiency was poor relative to that of the conventional vehicle from which it was derived, but this was attributed to the low efficiency of the oversized CVT and other inefficiencies in the drive train.

In the case of flywheel energy storage, the CVT can be used in place of the electrical transmission to provide a controlled power flow between the flywheel and vehicle drive. A CVT was used on the Parry rail vehicle shown in figure 2.7, and on the larger Parry vehicle which was operated in Bristol, as described in Chapter 7.

Amongst the many hybrid vehicles developed by Parry was the interesting arrangement shown in figure 2.9. This is unusual in that the transmission system is entirely mechanical. The arrangement has the advantage of low cost relative to electric transmission. However, continuing advances in power electronic control technology mean that the efficiency of electrical transmission is improving all the time, with up to 93% storage efficiency having been achieved in the CCM EMAFER system described in Chapter 3. Mechanical systems using CVTs, though much lower in cost, are unlikely to achieve this level of efficiency.

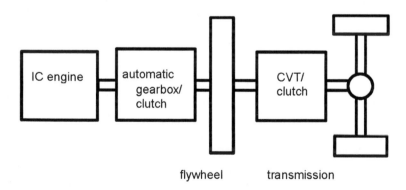

Figure 2.9:   Schematic arrangement of the Parry series mechanical hybrid drive
               with flywheel energy storage.

2.4 Parallel hybrid arrangements

A common form of the parallel hybrid consists of a diesel or petrol engine driving the wheels via a direct mechanical transmission, with supplementary power and regenerative braking being provided by a battery and an electric motor/generator unit, as illustrated in figure 2.10. As in most hybrid arrangements, the i.c. engine can be downsized by up to 60% depending on the vehicle type, and the energy storage capacity and efficiency. The criteria for sizing the engine and other components are discussed more fully in Chapter 5.

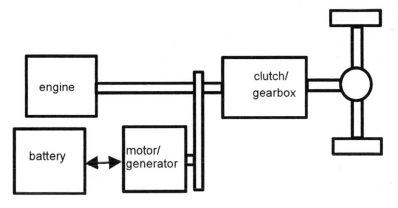

Figure 2.10: Parallel petrol engine/battery-electric hybrid arrangement.

The electric motor/generator has five functions:

1. to start the engine
2. to boost the engine power during acceleration
3. to absorb brake energy
4. to charge the battery
5. to supply vehicle auxiliaries

The motor/generator can supply power to the wheels as a motor, or can act as a generator to transmit power back to the battery, thereby effectively acting as a brake. The use of such regenerative braking is one of the major advantages of the hybrid.

The use of the motor/generator to start the primary engine not only removes the need for a conventional starter motor, but also enables rapid, quiet and smooth restarting, thus allowing the engine to be switched off when not needed. Most current automotive auxiliary systems operate on 12 V, whereas the traction motor will normally require a much higher voltage. A separate small alternator and battery may therefore sometimes be used to supply the 12 V auxiliaries.

2.4.1 The integrated motor assist approach

The electric motor/generator may be coupled to the engine via a belt drive, or by a mechanical gearing arrangement (as on the Toyota THS system), or may be integral with the engine, replacing the normal flywheel (as in the Honda IMA system). The Honda integrated system is very compact, and permits the use of a conventional gearbox and clutch, a feature that may be attractive to many potential drivers. Conventional mechanical transmissions are well developed and highly efficient. A disadvantage of this system is that the engine and generator must run at the same speed. Features of the Honda IMA system are described in Chapter 7. This arrangement now seems to be the preferred choice for the very 'mild' form of hybrid that offers only a small departure from a conventional vehicle.

2.4.2 Parallel arrangement with a mechanical torque splitting device

An alternative parallel battery hybrid arrangement is provided by the Toyota THS system. The system is shown schematically in figure 2.11. Here, an electric motor/generator and the i.c. engine are connected via a power splitting epicyclic gear unit. The gear unit is also connected to a second generator/motor, which is used to control the relative velocities of the engine and primary motor/generator.

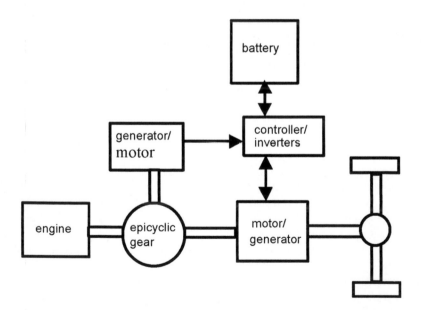

Figure 2.11: Parallel electric hybrid with an epicyclic power split device.

Figure 2.12 shows the mechanical arrangement in principle. The primary motor/generator is coupled directly to the final drive, and is connected to the outer ring gear of the epicyclic unit. The i.c. engine drives the carrier of the planetary gears in the unit, and the secondary generator/motor is connected to the inner sun gear. The torque applied by the secondary generator/motor is used to vary the effective gear ratio between the i.c. engine and the output shaft. The secondary generator may also be operated as a starter motor. This ingenious arrangement not only allows torque splitting, but also provides a continuously variable transmission (CVT) between the engine and the final drive train. The system also has the advantage that the i.c. engine torque and speed can be adjusted to be at the point of optimum efficiency throughout most of the drive cycle. The Toyota THS system has been under development since the 1970s, and features in the production Prius car. The Toyota system combines features of both series and parallel hybrids, and works in a combination of either or both modes, according to the operating conditions.

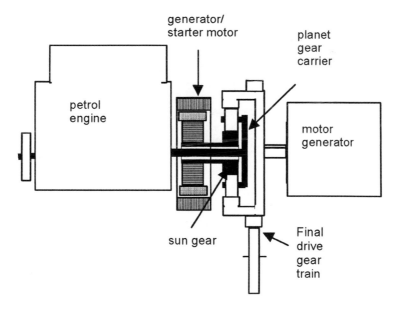

Figure 2.12:   The operating arrangement of the Toyota epicyclic torque-splitting gear system (after Bursa [2.3]).

2.4.3 Parallel hybrids with flywheels

It is a fairly straightforward task to devise a number of arrangements of either flywheel/battery or flywheel/i.c. engine. In the flywheel/battery arrangement, the flywheel speed variation is determined by the power required to be drawn from it, and the battery/electric motor becomes the prime mover. This represents an improvement on the pure battery electric vehicle, as it exploits the high specific power of the flywheel and its superior cycle life. The same epicyclic torque splitting arrangement can be used to provide a highly efficient mechanical coupling between the flywheel and output shafts.

In the case of a parallel flywheel/i.c. engine system, various mechanical transmission arrangements involving epicyclic ratio splitting units or CVTs have been proposed. Given the options of electric drives, planetary gears, CVTs, flywheels and batteries, in addition to conventional automotive transmission equipment, there are numerous possible configurations which could qualify as hybrid transmission.

2.5 Hydraulic systems

So far, mechanical and electrical transmission and energy storage systems have been described. Another option, namely hydraulic transmission, can also be considered in either a parallel or series arrangement. Hybrid arrangements using hydraulic transmissions are described in Chapter 3. There has as yet been no commercial exploitation of such systems.

2.6 The evolutionary process

Many different hybrid propulsion systems have been investigated, but it is not yet possible to isolate any one of them as the obvious winner, because component design is always improving. It may well be that different applications will favour different options. Factors that will influence the choice are production cost, reliability, cycle life, weight, compactness, flexibility, efficiency and noise. At present, parallel mechanical/electrical hybrid systems are favoured in car design because of their high efficiency, and ability to make use of well proven automotive transmission components. However, series electric hybrid configurations may well emerge as the preferred option for larger urban passenger transit vehicles, where the vehicle duty cycle can reap practical advantages from the electric transmission. Low noise, smooth stepless transmission, and the ability to operate in purely electric zero-emissions mode provide great benefits in inner city areas.

2.7 References

[2.1]   Crosse, Jesse, Daimler Chrysler charts a third way for hybrids. *FT Automotive World,* Financial Times Business Ltd, December 1999, p23.

[2.2]   Collie, M. J. (editor), *Electric and Hybrid Vehicles*, Noyes Data Corp., New Jersey, USA, 1979.

[2.3]   Bursa, M., Toyota's double-drive hybrid power train, *ISATA Magazine*, May 1997.

Chapter 3

ENERGY STORAGE OPTIONS

3.1 The requirement for energy storage

The required energy storage capacity of hybrid vehicles is generally much smaller than that of a pure battery electric vehicle. In hybrid vehicles intended for urban use, the prime mover is normally sized to provide the mean energy requirements of the journey. The storage device is used to smooth out the variations in power demand, and provide sufficient energy for a limited amount of pure zero emissions operation. In mild hybrids, the stored energy is primarily used to assist the prime mover during acceleration and hill climbing, and to absorb brake energy during deceleration. Brake energy absorption places a significant demand on any energy storage facility in terms of its ability to absorb high levels of input power, since the power dissipated by friction brakes in a conventional vehicle during deceleration can easily exceed the maximum power output of the engine. This means that although the energy storage capacity required may be low, the specific power requirement is high. As described below, this produces considerable technical difficulties if batteries are to be used as the storage medium.

3.2 The advantages of energy storage

In addition to the opportunity for brake energy recovery already mentioned, energy storage effectively acts as a buffer between the prime mover power and the vehicle demand power, making them largely independent. This allows for the use of a wide variety of primary power sources, as they are not required to respond to rapid changes in traction power demand. Possible prime movers include gas turbines, high efficiency internal combustion engines and fuel cells. These options permit the use of a range of alternative fuels, including hydrogen. The use of a fuel cell would result in the same quiet, vibration-free performance currently obtained from battery vehicles, but without the range limitation. The stable power demand would allow the use of a reformer, which would permit the use of liquid fuels such as methanol. The options for prime movers are considered in detail in Chapter 4.

3.3 Characteristics of energy storage devices

In the international metric (S.I.) unit system, energy is expressed in Joules (J), but it is a common practice in the electrical engineering industry to give energy in terms of Watt-hours (Wh). In this book, we use the approved coherent S.I. units, but when discussing batteries, we will also quote battery specific energy in Wh/kg, since this makes comparison with published data easier. It may be noted that since a Watt is a Joule per second, 1 Wh = 3.6 kJ.

The important characteristics of energy storage in hybrid vehicle design are:

Energy density: the energy capacity per unit volume of the storage system: (units kJ/m^3 or Wh/m^3).

Specific energy: the energy capacity per unit mass: (units kJ/kg or Wh/kg).

Power density: the available power output per unit volume: (units W/m^3).

Specific power: the available power output per unit mass: (units W/kg).

Note that in hybrid vehicles, the power flows both in and out, so that the power density and specific power should be quoted for charge as well as discharge. For most batteries, the maximum charge power is far less than the available discharge power.

Storage efficiency:

$$\frac{\text{energy available on discharge}}{\text{energy required for recharging to the same state}} \times \ 100\%$$

Permitted depth of discharge (DOD): the energy discharge allowed, as a percentage of total energy capacity, before recharge. Note that this is rarely over 80% and for batteries it may be as little as 20% in order to preserve battery life. This is, of course, a key determinant of energy storage capacity.

Charge time: the minimum time required to recharge from the (permitted) discharged state.

Cycle life: The life of the energy storage system measured in the number of charge/discharge cycles that it can sustain.

Self-discharge rate: Most energy storage systems will lose energy over a period of time. Flywheels, ultracapacitors and all types of rechargeable batteries suffer from this problem. Some of the more advanced battery designs are particularly poor in this respect. The self-discharge rate is the time taken for energy stored in the device to reduce to a specified percentage of the full charge. In the case of batteries, this is normally taken as the 80% depth of discharge (80% DOD).

3.4 Batteries

Batteries have been chosen as the storage device in the first generation of hybrid cars, and in most of the hybrid bus systems.

The attractions of batteries are that:

1. their technology is well developed (for some types)
2. there is a considerable body of experience in their use, deriving from many years of operation of electric vehicle fleets
3. they have no moving parts
4. their safety record is generally good, although some newer types do represent a significant potential hazard.

Batteries also have some major disadvantages for hybrid propulsion systems:

1. They tend to have a limited cycle life, particularly if subjected to repeated heavy current flows on discharge and charge, or repeated deep discharges.
2. They have a much lower specific power than a conventional i.c. engine, and thus tend to make the vehicle heavy.
3. They have an even lower specific power on charge, and this, rather than the specific energy, may determine the size of battery required.
4. High-performance batteries are relatively expensive.
5. Their storage efficiency (energy output/energy input) is relatively low and decreases with higher power flow.

Due to the continuing interest in the development of zero emission vehicles, a considerable amount of research and development work has been undertaken on batteries. The lead was taken in North America by the United States Advanced Battery Consortium (USABC). This was superseded by the United States Council for Automotive Research (USCAR), which in turn co-operated with the US Government to form the Partnership for a New Generation of Vehicles (PNGV). Some progress has been made, particularly with the development of newer battery types such as the nickel metal-hydride (NiMH).

Compared to pure battery electric vehicles (BEVs), hybrid electric vehicles (HEVs) impose some even more severe operational constraints on batteries. This is because the peak power requirements are roughly the same for both types of vehicle, but for a hybrid, the battery should be relatively small and light (a high total vehicle mass will tend to eliminate the advantages of the hybrid system). The hybrid vehicle battery will therefore have to work at a much higher specific power (power to weight ratio) than for a BEV, and this will greatly reduce both the life and the efficiency. The cycling will also be more intense on a hybrid vehicle. On a BEV, the battery operates one major cycle of charging and discharging during a journey, with some much smaller cycles being superimposed by alternating periods of acceleration, cruise and regenerative braking. In a hybrid, because of the smaller capacity, the battery would suffer a major discharge and charge for each of these cycles of acceleration, cruise and braking. For this reason, battery hybrids often carry 5 times the necessary battery load, in order to restrict the depth of discharge to 20%, and to reduce the maximum cell current.

3.4.1 Problems of comparisons

Before attempting to set out the comparative advantages of some of the various batteries, it is necessary to outline the difficulties inherent in such comparisons.

1. The characteristics required of the battery will depend on the type of hybrid. The mild hybrid and the large storage capacity hybrid will have similar requirements in terms of the amount of power involved in regenerative braking, but because the mild hybrid will have a much smaller battery, it will require a correspondingly higher specific power.
2. The performance characteristics of the battery will change with time. The performance of all batteries gradually deteriorates. The characteristics will even change during a journey, due to changes in the battery temperature.
3. The total energy capacity of the battery is not available to be extracted on a regular basis, since this would rapidly destroy the battery.
4. The amount of energy that can be extracted depends on the output power. Less energy is available at high power output than at low power, because more energy is lost in heat. Figure 3.1 shows the variation in the amount of useful energy extracted from a typical lead-acid battery with the time taken to drop to 20% of the maximum charge (80% depth of discharge). The energy output is expressed as a percentage of the drop in charge. It will be seen that the useful energy obtained in an 8 hour discharge is twice as much as that for a 1 hour discharge. This means that for the fast discharge rate, the battery needs to be twice as heavy to produce the same energy output as at the low discharge rate.

3.4.2 Basis of comparison of available energy: the C factors

In order to provide a basis of comparison, battery manufacturers often quote a figure for the amount of useful energy that can be extracted by discharging the battery by 80% (that is down to 20% of the original maximum charge) during a period of 5 hours. (A proportion of the original charge is always lost as waste heat). Discharge to 80% DOD in 5 hours is known as the C5 rate. Unfortunately, in traction batteries, the rate of discharge in normal use is often much greater than this, and varies considerably during the journey. A much more relevant figure would be that for a fast discharge of around 1 hour (C1 rate) or less. A battery with a good energy output at the C5 rate may well have a relatively poor C1 value. In this chapter, the typical specific energy values given are for the C5 condition except where otherwise stated. This is simply because of the availability of C5 data, and general scarcity of C1 data.

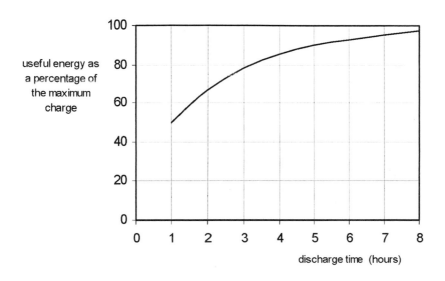

Figure 3.1: Variation in the amount of useful energy that can be extracted from a typical lead-acid battery with time to discharge to 20% of maximum.

3.4.3 The importance of storage efficiency

If brake energy recovery is the prime purpose of adopting hybrid technology, then energy storage efficiency (useful energy output/energy input during charging) is critical. In order to verify this, a sensitivity test was carried out by the authors using the SIMTRIP vehicle model [3.1]. The subject of the test was a large saloon car undergoing a start stop cycle over a 500 m distance in urban conditions. The following assumptions were made:

Mass of vehicle	1.3 tonnes	Frontal area	2 m^2
Distance	500 m	Drag coefficient	0.35
Transmission efficiency	90%	Rolling resistance coefficient	0.012
Maximum acceleration/deceleration	3 m/s^2	Energy storage standing losses	0 kW
Traction power limit	75 kW	Prime mover power	23 kW
Gradient	0%	Maximum speed	50 km/h

The results are shown in figure 3.2 and graphically in figure 3.3. The fuel saving indicated is theoretical, and is strongly dependent on the control strategy used. Any changes in transmission efficiency and any additional weight due to the energy storage (which would be large with battery storage) have been ignored and self-discharge effects have been neglected. The purpose of this analysis is solely to indicate the sensitivity to storage efficiency.

Energy storage efficiency %	Energy used kJ	Fuel savings relative to non-hybrid %
100	151	42
81	193	26
64	223	14
49	243	6
Maximum kinetic energy		125 kJ
Wheel losses		76 kJ
Aerodynamic losses		37 kJ

Figure 3.2: Predicted effect of energy storage efficiency on fuel consumption.

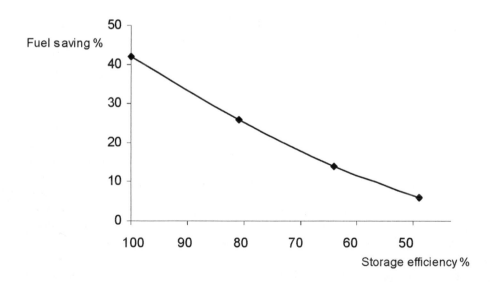

Figure 3.3:   Sensitivity of fuel savings to energy storage efficiency.

3.5 Types of battery and their suitability for hybrid applications

3.5.1 The lead-acid battery

In automotive applications, the most common form of energy storage, apart from the fuel tank, is the lead-acid battery. These are mass produced on a world-wide scale, are relatively low in cost, and are readily available. The United States Advanced Battery Consortium (USABC) and its later manifestations specifically excluded development work on the lead-acid battery, which has a poor specific energy, and was thus considered to be unlikely to provide the kind of performance that would be required for viable BEVs. To counter this move, the American lead-acid battery manufacturers responded by forming their own Advanced Lead Acid Battery Consortium (ALABC). Their efforts have led to significant improvements in the performance and practicality of the lead-acid battery with developments such as advanced sealed types, and the valve regulated lead-acid battery (VRLA). These advanced lead-acid batteries are still not satisfactory for long-range BEVs, but they seem likely to find a place in hybrid propulsion.

Several experimental and development hybrid vehicles have used lead-acid batteries as the energy storage device. Operators of such vehicles are, however, finding that the advantage in fuel consumption over the equivalent conventional vehicle can be disappointingly small. The experience of such operators is described more fully in Chapter 7. Nevertheless, because of its widespread use and low cost, it is convenient to take the lead-acid battery as the reference datum against which to compare other forms of energy storage. The performance of lead-acid batteries varies considerably according to the method of construction, and advances are still taking place. The data in figure 3.4 are based on a study of a large number of published reports, and indicate the range of variation. The lead-acid battery has a fair performance in terms of energy storage and power output when new, but this deteriorates during its lifetime.

Energy density (J/litre)	960
Specific energy at C5 (Wh/kg)	22 -50
(kJ/kg)	79 - 180
Specific power (W/kg)	75 - 150
Storage efficiency (%)	60 -75
Charge time (hours)	8
Cycle life	400 -1200

Figure 3.4:   Characteristics of lead-acid batteries.

In hybrid vehicle operation, if only the minimum requisite amount of energy storage were carried, then each start stop cycle would constitute one cycle of battery life. A vehicle can undergo hundreds of such cycles per day, and this could reduce the battery's life to weeks. In lead-acid battery hybrid vehicles, such cycling is normally restricted to below 10% depth of discharge. At this level, the batteries can sustain 50 to 100 times as many cycles, thus prolonging the battery life. The down side of this is that 10 times more battery weight must be carried than would otherwise be necessary.

The critical factor in hybrid vehicles is the brake energy recovery requirement. Energy is dissipated in the friction brakes of a conventional car at a rate of up to 150 kW. To absorb power at this rate would require nearly 2 tonnes of batteries, but fortunately, in practice, heavy braking at this level does not occur frequently, so about half this weight of batteries would normally be sufficient. Regenerative braking produces a further gain in operational efficiency, by reducing wear on the brake pads.

Conventional designs of lead-acid batteries, with their relatively low values of specific energy and power, are not well suited for application in vehicles, which require a high specific power. Future designs may go some way to overcoming this problem, and development is underway of special lead-acid batteries for hybrid applications with a specific energy of only 20 Wh/kg but a specific output power of up to 750 W/kg. This would reduce the weight of the required battery pack by a factor of 5. With storage efficiency unlikely to exceed 80%, however, the energy savings from brake energy recovery would still be limited.

The performance of lead-acid batteries is temperature sensitive, and for automotive applications temperature control is necessary. Despite its limitations, some manufacturers of hybrid vehicles still favour the lead-acid battery because of its low cost and ease of maintenance. Toyota, who pioneered the mild hybrid vehicle, used nickel-metal hydride batteries for its first production vehicles, but has moved to lead-acid batteries for some later models.

3.5.2 Nickel-cadmium (Ni-Cd) batteries

These batteries are now in common use in small domestic appliances and efforts have been made to develop them for automotive use. They have the advantage over lead-acid batteries of a much higher specific power and thus lighter weight. Ni-Cd batteries can have anything up to three times the specific power of a conventional lead-acid battery. They also have a higher cycle life. Disadvantages include the higher cost, particularly the cost of recycling cadmium, which is highly toxic, and poor charge retention. A 30% charge loss per 48 hours is typical. Poor charge retention is not so important for hybrid vehicles as it is for BEVs, because the prime mover can readily recharge the battery. However, there remains the problem of starting the vehicle after it has been left idle for a number of weeks. A secondary lead-acid starter battery would probably be needed.

Another problem with Ni-Cd batteries is that they suffer from a pronounced 'memory' effect. This means that if the battery is regularly topped up without being allowed to discharge fully, the amount of charge that it can take decreases; Ni-Cd batteries need to be fully discharged occasionally. In vehicle traction applications, Nickel Cadmium battery development has been largely overtaken by introduction of the superior nickel-metal hydride (Ni-MH) batteries described below.

3.5.3 Nickel-Metal Hydride (Ni-MH) batteries

Ni-MH batteries are finding increasing use in small domestic equipment such as cameras and mobile telephones. An advanced version of this battery type was selected for the first two large-scale production hybrid cars, the Toyota Prius, and the Honda Insight. The specific power is similar to that of the Ni-Cd battery, but the specific energy is higher. The charge rate of small domestic cells is lower than for the Ni-Cd battery, but the advanced designs used in automotive applications have produced acceptable charging rates. A further problem is the rather higher temperature sensitivity, and in vehicle applications, temperature control is necessary. Memory effect is less of a problem, and charge retention is superior to that of the Ni-Cd but still inferior to the lead-acid battery. Self-discharge rates of around a 25% loss in four weeks are typical for automotive traction batteries. Even this relatively low rate could cause starting problems if the vehicle were laid up for more than a month. The Ni-MH is intrinsically safe. The components are not toxic like those in the Ni-Cd, but nickel is an expensive and rather scarce resource. This results in the main disadvantage of the Ni-MH battery, which is its high cost. This is typically between five and ten times that of a lead-acid battery.

3.5.4 Lithium-ion (Li-ion) and Lithium Solid Polymer (Li-SP) batteries

Lithium-ion batteries show considerable potential, with specific power values of up to 800 W/kg being reported (compared to around 150 W/kg for a lead-acid battery). The closely related Li-SP batteries show specific power of up to 500 W/kg and specific energies of up to 150 Wh/kg, and a reported storage efficiency of up to 95%. Development of these batteries for hybrid vehicle use is continuing.

3.5.5 High temperature batteries: Sodium Sulphur (Na-S), Sodium-Nickel Chloride (Na-NiCl) and Lithium Sulphur (Li-S)

During the 1980s and early 1990s considerable research effort was directed towards Na-S batteries, which use molten sodium and sulphur, and therefore need to be kept at continuously high temperatures of between 250 and 350°C. For pure BEV operation, the high specific energy of around 90-100 Wh/kg and high cycle life were sufficiently attractive to encourage development. However, the need to maintain a continuous high temperature (even when not in use), the hazard represented by molten sodium, and the poor charge retention resulted in a waning of enthusiasm in the late 1990s. Similar problems were encountered for the other high temperature batteries. For hybrid vehicles, where high specific energy is not the highest priority, it is unlikely that they will find a use.

3.5.6 Nickel-Iron (Ni-Fe) batteries

These are comparable in performance with Ni-Cd batteries except that the storage efficiency is poorer at only around 60%. This, coupled with high maintenance and high cost, has led to a loss of interest for vehicle applications.

3.5.7 Nickel-Zinc (Ni-Zn) batteries

Ni-Zn battery performance is similar to that of Ni-Cd batteries, except that at present, their cycle life is reputedly poor at around 300. There seems to be little enthusiasm for further development of this battery type for automotive use.

3.5.8 Zinc-bromine (Zn-Br) batteries

This is a new technology currently being investigated, but this battery type has a number of disadvantages including a low storage efficiency of around 70%. Their optimum operating temperature is around $40°C$, and they typically self-discharge by around 30% in 48 hours. They also have a poor cycle life of around 500. For these reasons they are not presently considered as a candidate for hybrid vehicle applications.

3.5.9 Nickel Hydrogen (Ni-H$_2$) batteries

Impressive claims have been made for this type, including almost infinite longevity, and an extremely high cycle life of over 60,000 cycles at moderate energy extraction rates. It has been used as a power source in satellite communication systems. Despite these features, there is as yet, little evidence that much effort is going into developing this battery for automotive propulsion. The cost of existing units is high.

3.6 Summary of battery performance

Trying to obtain meaningful comparisons of the performance of the various battery types is difficult. Many of them are still under development, and the extremes of performance may be achieved from complex arrangements that are not suited to automotive applications. As mentioned previously, the performance may deteriorate rapidly with age, and a high power output may be associated with a very short cycle life. In figure 3.5 we have attempted to show figures for advanced versions of current developments. These may become rapidly outdated in some cases, and the table should only be taken as a rough guide. The values are based on data obtained from a large number of sources, including Atkin and Storey [3.2] who in turn used numerous sources.

	Lead-acid	Ni-Cd	Ni-MH	Na-S	Ni-Fe	Zn-Br	Li-SP
Specific energy (Wh/kg)	50	55	75	110	45	75	150
(kJ/kg)	180	198	270	396	162	270	540
Energy density (kJ/litre)	960	1200	1800	553	720	360	360
Specific power (W/kg) at C5	150	200	200	170	170	100	500
Storage Efficiency (%)	77	75	75	90	60	70	95
Self discharge in 2 days (%)	5	30	10	30	25	30	-
Normal life (years)	4.5	5	5	5	6	4	5
Normal charge time (hours)	8	5	10	4	10	6	5
Cycle life (at 80% DOD)	600 - 1200	2000	1500	1500	2000	500	300

Figure 3.5:   Comparisons of the performance of advanced versions of various battery types.

3.7 Other forms of energy storage

Though batteries are widely used as the storage element in hybrid electric vehicles they have not yet proved very satisfactory, because of their limited cycle life, low power density and poor storage efficiency. This has led to the need to carry an excessive weight of batteries and to a limited ability to recover brake energy. Other forms of energy storage under evaluation for vehicle application are:

- the hydraulic accumulator
- compressed air
- the flywheel
- the ultracapacitor.

3.7.1 The hydraulic accumulator

A hybrid system based on hydraulic transmission and storage is shown in figure 3.6. The energy storage is provided by way of a hydraulic accumulator comprising an oil-filled pressure vessel in which energy is absorbed or released by elastic objects contained within the vessel. These objects can be in the form of compressible spheres filled with nitrogen. The power transmission is by way of hydraulic motors, which act as compressors for power reversal. By employing hydraulic motors, the power transmission can also be hydraulic. This form of energy storage combines a high power density with a good cycle life at relatively low cost.

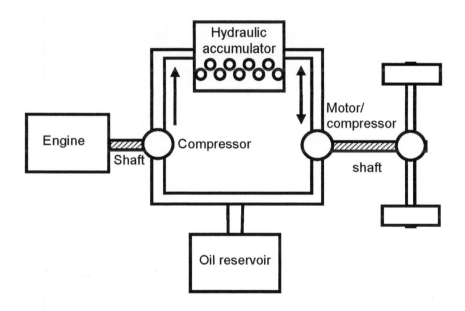

Figure 3.6: Series hybrid arrangement with hydraulic transmission.

A hydraulic transmission and energy storage system was developed for a bus by MAN in the 1980s. The Hydrobus 3 used a 0.75 MJ hydraulic accumulator in conjunction with a torque splitting differential gear train, which, like the Prius, provided continuously variable transmission and a mixed parallel/series form of transmission. This allowed the prime mover to operate with direct mechanical transmission under some conditions. The energy storage capacity, though small, was sufficient to provide regenerative braking. A diesel engine was used, and because of the small amount of stored energy available, it was of the same type and power rating (150 kW) as that in a conventional bus. This vehicle was thus an example of a very 'mild' hybrid. The manufacturers claimed fuel savings of up to 33% compared to a corresponding conventional bus with automatic transmission. In addition MAN also experimented with a hydraulically driven flywheel with a maximum capacity of 1 MJ at 7330 rpm. Some of the work on the MAN buses is described by Hagin [3.3]. Volvo Flygmotor in Sweden has also conducted field tests on a 16 ton diesel/flywheel hybrid bus with pure series hydraulic transmission. This vehicle used an 8.2 MJ hydraulically driven flywheel rather than a hydraulic accumulator. The flywheel weighed 330 kg and rotated at up to 10,000 rpm. The output power of the flywheel could supplement the 100 kW output of a diesel engine, to give a maximum total output of 225 kW, which compares favourably with the 160 kW available with the diesel engine of the original bus with conventional diesel/mechanical transmission. The system was robust and performed well, showing fuel consumption improvements of 15% to 25% compared to a conventional diesel bus with mechanical transmission.

The results of the trials of both the MAN and Volvo were highly encouraging in terms of the fuel savings obtained, but neither project has yet resulted in a commercial production vehicle. The cost advantage of hydraulic over electrical transmission is rather outweighed by the disadvantages of higher weight and volume, and somewhat higher noise levels.

3.7.2 Compressed air storage

There has been some media interest in reported attempts to use a compressed air energy storage system for vehicle propulsion. Available technical details of this development are thin, but it is clearly theoretically possible to use compressed air to drive either a reciprocating motor or a turbine directly, with no combustion. This is a pneumatic analogy of battery electric storage, and power reversal is similarly possible for brake energy recovery.

The problem with compressed air storage systems, apart from any practical mechanical difficulties, lies in their apparently poor levels of specific energy and energy density. Assuming adiabatic expansion, it is a simple matter to show that even with storage pressures as high as 350 atmospheres (the pressure envisaged for compressed hydrogen storage), and pressure vessels using modern materials, the theoretical maximum specific energy available is around 16 kJ/kg, which is only around 1/10 of the value obtainable from a lead-acid battery. The energy density is similarly less than 1/10 of the value obtainable from a battery. This means that compressed air would be unsuitable as the sole source of power in a vehicle. However, a specific energy of 16 kJ/kg is comparable with that obtained from a flywheel or ultracapacitor so, as with these devices, compressed air storage could be a viable option for hybrid vehicles, particularly as it should be capable of producing high specific power and a good cycle life. There has been little published information of the current state of the technical development of such devices.

3.7.3 Flywheel energy storage

Flywheels are becoming of increasing interest in hybrid vehicle design, particularly for larger passenger transit vehicles. This is because of their advantage over batteries in terms of cycle life, power density, rapid charge rate and storage efficiency. The energy density is primarily related to the speed of rotation. Increasing the speed of rotation produces improved specific energy, but increases the potential safety hazard, and also the cost, since special bearings and high strength materials are required.

Several companies have developed practical flywheel storage systems, and in Europe, the companies CCM in the Netherlands and Magnet Motor in Southern Germany have accumulated considerable experience with the running of production flywheel-electric hybrid vehicles, as described in Chapter 7.

The CCM flywheels are constructed of composite material and designed to rotate at speeds of up to 15,000 rpm. They rotate in a vacuum containment, and incorporate an integral motor/generator. The motor is designed so that the central armature is stationary and the permanent magnet excitation rotates with the flywheel. This means that the armature windings can be fed electronically rather than by brushes and slip rings. These flywheels are operated with regenerative electronic drives of modern design, and energy storage efficiencies of up to 93% have been achieved. Higher speed designs have been tested but there remains the problem of charging and discharging energy in a controlled manner at the required rate and with the required efficiency. Figure 3.7 shows the CCM flywheel unit [3.4 and 3.5]. This has a capacity of 4 kWh (14.4 MJ), a charge and discharge power rating of 300 kW and a maximum speed of 15,000 rpm.

People who are unfamiliar with flywheel systems often raise concerns about possible gyroscopic effects, but potential problems in this respect have been avoided by Magnet Motor and CCM by mounting the flywheels with their axis vertical and placing them in a cardanic suspension system as shown in figure 3.7. Precession effects simply cause the unit to move within its suspension frame. It is practical to allow such movement, because the power inputs and outputs of the flywheel units are entirely electrical.

Another concern expressed about flywheels is that of safety, but many years of practical experience in operating flywheel vehicles (as described in Chapter 7) has revealed that such fears are unfounded. The CCM flywheel has had an exhaustive safety-testing programme. In an ultimate test, the flywheel was accelerated to twice the specified maximum speed without mishap. In order to test the effect of a failure, holes had to be drilled into the flywheel near its perimeter and the test repeated.

Figure 3.7:   A CCM flywheel mounted in its cardanic suspension.
(Photo courtesy of CCM.)

As shown in figure 3.8, the result was that disintegration did occur, but the effect was contained. Because of the composite material construction of the flywheel, the resultant residue was a fine powder distributed within the containment. The energy was absorbed as heat.

Figure 3.8:   The effects of artificially induced failure in a CCM composite flywheel. The wheel disintegrated, but was fully contained. (Photo courtesy of CCM.)

The original CCM flywheel was developed over a period of about 10 years and was tested and demonstrated in a converted trolleybus, as described in Chapter 7. The energy storage efficiency, at 93%, has resulted in fuel savings of up to 35% compared to a standard diesel bus in urban driving conditions. The prime mover is a 2 litre Audi car engine which, under these conditions, operates at a steady 35 kW.

Figure 3.9 shows approximate relative figures for energy density, power density and cycle life for the CCM flywheel unit in comparison with lead-acid batteries currently used in hybrid electric vehicles. A flywheel hybrid system for a light rail vehicle is described by Jefferson *et al.* [3.6].

Property	Ratio relative to the lead-acid battery
Energy density	0.025
Specific energy	0.25
Output power density	6
Specific output power	7
Cycle life	1000
Recharge rate	240

Figure 3.9: Properties of flywheel energy storage relative to the lead-acid battery.

Increasing the speed of rotation produces improved specific energy. The Magnet Motor MDS K3 flywheel unit has a specific energy of 18 kJ/kg at a rotational speed of 12,000 rpm while the MDS K6, which rotates at 21,000 rpm, achieves a specific energy of 55 kJ/kg. For a given flywheel, the energy increases as the square of the rotational speed, but the higher speed may require a stronger and heavier casing, so the increase in specific energy will not generally follow a square law.

Very much higher specific energy values can be obtained with more exotic designs, and in 1994 Riley [3.7] described a flywheel system being developed by AFS (American Flywheel Systems) using a rotational speed of up to 200,000 rpm to produce a specific energy of some 970 kJ/kg. Practical considerations, cost and safety concerns have however led flywheel-based hybrid vehicle producers to opt for much lower operational speeds, as above. In any case, in hybrid vehicle applications, energy density is not of critical importance; the amount of stored energy required is much smaller than for a pure battery-electric vehicle.

From a practical point of view, important positive features of flywheel systems are the high cycle life, high power density, good storage efficiency and short recharge time. For a flywheel system, the storage efficiency, potentially over 90%, is largely set by the efficiency of the transmission. The storage efficiency of conventional batteries tends to be below 60% and the low recharge rates are proving to be a major disadvantage in electric vehicle operation, and they allow only partial brake energy recovery. Flywheels have a much shorter energy retention time than a battery, but this does not present a problem in hybrid vehicles. For a flywheel, energy charge and discharge rates should be equal, and sufficiently short for automotive purposes.

3.7.4 Ultracapacitors

The electrical capacitor, or condenser, as the device was previously known, was developed as a highly efficient means of absorbing and storing fairly small quantities of electrical charge. The capacity for energy storage is rather low but the main purpose of these devices is as a passive component to absorb small electrical disturbances or high frequency signals. They can withstand fairly large voltages and current pulses and have a high cycle life. Their storage capacity is normally rated as the electrical charge stored per unit voltage applied, and has the units of Farads (F).

The term 'supercapacitor' is commonly used to describe double layer capacitors that have a higher specific energy than conventional capacitors and have capacitance values ranging from 1-1000 F. The term 'ultracapacitor' is used for capacitors that have a capacitance value exceeding 1000 F. The energy storage capacity depends not only on the capacitance but also on the maximum voltage the device can stand. In fact:

$$\text{Energy stored} = 0.5 \times \text{capacitance} \times \text{voltage}^2 \tag{3.1}$$

The simplest form of capacitor comprises a pair of parallel plates. The amount of charge, and thus energy stored, depends on the area of the plates and the distance between them. For high capacity, the area should be large and the gap as small as possible without the risk of a short circuit. In an ultracapacitor the gap is filled with an electrolyte, normally of solid polymer [3.8]. The 'plates' then become electrodes, as in a battery, except that no chemical reaction is involved, only some ionisation on the electrode surface. The electrodes are made of a porous material, normally activated carbon, which has a very high specific surface area (>2000 m^2/g). Whichever the direction of the applied voltage, one of the boundaries between the electrode and electrolyte blocks any charge transfer, so that charge is accumulated. The high capacitance results from the large effective surface area of the electrodes, and the fineness of the boundary layer between the electrolyte and the electrode, which is blocking the charge transfer.

As reported by Jost [3.9] in 1996, the American Department of Energy, Idaho National Engineering developed a 3 volt ultracapacitor of 2.3 kF with a specific energy of 18 kJ/kg. A number of devices with similar performance have been developed elsewhere, and are now commercially available.

In spite of the large capacitance, the low operating voltage (normally around 2-3 V) means that the energy storage capacity is quite low. However, as with a conventional capacitor, the charge and discharge rate is almost unrestricted, and the specific power is thus very high. Because no chemical reactions take place, there is little deterioration in performance with use, so the cycle life is very much higher than for a battery. The high specific power and cycle life, required for hybrid vehicle applications, are key features of ultracapacitors as energy storage devices.

Figure 3.10 compares typical performance figures for the lead-acid battery, the flywheel and the ultracapacitor. The specific power for the battery only relates to discharge and is much lower for charge, hence the long charge time. In the case of the ultracapacitor (and the flywheel), the specific power is limited only by the capacity of the interface by which the power is transmitted to or from the device.

	Lead-acid	Flywheel	Ultracapacitor
Specific energy (Wh/kg) (kJ/kg)	50 180	5-15 18-55	3 – 5 11-18
Specific power (W/kg)	150	500	300 – 500
Storage efficiency (%)	77	93	80 – 90
Normal charge time (hours)	8	Unrestricted	Unrestricted
Cycle life	600 –1200	>1,000,000	> 100,000

Figure 3.10:   Comparison of properties of lead-acid battery, flywheel and ultracapacitor.

In an ultracapacitor, the energy can, in theory, be discharged almost instantly, by shorting the terminals. Indeed, ultracapacitors are used where instant pulses of high power are required, and the potential for such high power pulses does raise some safety concerns. In a hybrid vehicle, however, the power has to be carefully controlled, and effective safeguards must be incorporated to ensure that sudden discharge cannot occur. The difference in operation between an ultracapacitor and a battery is that during normal operation, the voltage on a battery remains almost constant, whereas, as an ultracapacitor is discharged, the voltage drops according to equation (3.1).   (Energy = $0.5 \times$ capacitance $\times$ (voltage)^2).   This means that to interface the device with a fixed DC link, as in the arrangement shown in figure 2.4 (Chapter 2), a voltage converter is required to convert the varying ultracapacitor voltage to the fixed DC link voltage.   This will need to be a complex piece of power electronic equipment whose cost depends on its power capacity.   It is this capacity which determines the specific power of the storage system.   In order to get the right balance between specific energy and specific power for automotive applications, a combination of battery and ultracapacitor may be required.   In this case, both devices will need their own power controller.

The use of ultracapacitors with a 1 kW output was investigated by Davies *et al.* [3.8], and considerable progress with practical application in hybrid vehicles has been made by Honda, who used this method of energy storage for the advanced demonstrator version of the Honda IMA system in their JVX model, a forerunner of the Insight. Ultracapacitors are now gradually emerging from their development stage and products are on the market. However, the price is high and the specific energy still rather low, meaning that excessive space is required to house the energy storage needed. Future development may result in ultracapacitors becoming the favoured form of energy storage in hybrid electric vehicles.

3.8 Preferred storage options

In the first generation of hybrid vehicles, the lead-acid battery was the preferred energy storage device. However, for buses and light rail vehicles, flywheel-based systems have shown distinct advantages in terms of efficiency and reliability, as described in Chapter 7.

Thus far, small mild hybrid cars have also used batteries, with the most successful vehicles adopting the more advanced nickel metal-hydride type. There has however been some interest in the use of ultracapacitors for these vehicles, and these devices have distinct advantages over the battery in terms of cycle life and power density.

Other storage devices such as elastic polymer based arrangements, and the hydraulic and pneumatic devices described here have been under investigation, but there is currently no clear indication of their becoming serious contenders.

3.9 References

[3.1]   Jefferson, C. M. and Ackerman, M., A flywheel variator energy storage system, *Energy Conversion and Management*, Vol. 37, No. 10, pp. 1481-1491, 1996.

[3.2]   Atkin, G. and Storey, J., *Electric Vehicles: Prospects for battery-, fuel-cell and hybrid-powered vehicles,* FT Automotive, Financial Times Business Ltd, London, ISBN 1-84083-047-6, 1998.

[3.3]   Hagin, F., Regenerative braking systems for city buses, *Proceedings of the 20th Intersociety Conversion Conference (IECEC)*, August 1985, Miami.

[3.4]   Smits, E., Huisman, H. and Thoolen, F., A hybrid city bus using an electro mechanical accumulator for power demand smoothing. *Proceedings of the European Power Electronics Conference*, Vol. 4, Trondheim, 1997.

[3.5]   Huisman, H., Smits, E. J. F. M., Knaapen, R. J. W. and Thoolen, F. J. M., Using the Emafer flywheel for power demand smoothing in the ULEV-TAP light rail vehicle. *Proceedings of the European Power Electronics Conference*, Vol. 4, Trondheim, 1997. EPE-99, Lausanne, 1999.

[3.6]   Jefferson, C. M., Ackerman M. and Coveney V. A., Hybrid flywheel
         propulsion system for rail vehicles, *Proceedings of 27th ISATA*, Aachen,
         October 1994.
[3.7]   Riley, Robert Q., *Alternative Cars in the 21st Century*, SAE, ISBN 1-
         56091 519-6, 1994, p. 246.
[3.8]   Davies, T. S., Jefferson, C. M., Larson, N. and Nouri, K., DC-DC power
         conversion for a supercapacitor energy storage system, *Proceedings of
         the 31st UPEC*, Iralkio, September 1996, Vol. 1, pp. 289-292.
[3.9]   Jost, K., Alternative energy storage, *Automotive Engineering*, Nov.
         1996, pp. 35-36.

Chapter 4

CHOICE OF PRIME MOVER

The prime mover on a hybrid system is usually required to operate at a more constant load and speed than in a conventional vehicle, and thus the choice of power unit is wider. Devices such as gas turbines, which are normally considered unsuitable for land vehicles, become serious contenders. In this chapter we will discuss the pros and cons of a number of prime movers in the context of their suitability for use in hybrid propulsion systems. Due to the continuous process of development, the relative strengths and weaknesses of the various rival forms of prime mover change from time to time, but over the longer term, the important characteristic differences are determined by fundamental physical factors.

4.1 Meeting the emission requirements

The various European emission standards are given in Chapter 1. It is expected that EURO III emission limits can be met by both diesel engines and spark ignition engines using conventional propulsion systems. In the case of HGVs (heavy goods vehicles), there is a feeling that manufacturers could be tempted to raise the nominal power of their engines in order to reduce the emission figures, since these are expressed in grams/kWh.

It is not clear how future limits, EURO IV and V, can be met by internal combustion engines in conventional vehicles, which is a strong reason for moving to hybrid designs. For HGVs, the emission limits would need to be based on the power delivered to the wheels. There is a proposal, however, for specific vehicle types such as buses, to have emission limits expressed in grams per km, as for passenger cars.

We will now consider the pros and cons of the various options.

4.2 The spark ignition petrol (gasoline) engine

The spark ignition engine has been the preferred motor for domestic vehicle propulsion since the earliest days of motoring. Though normally run on petrol (gasoline), it can be used with a wide range of gases and volatile hydrocarbons such as alcohols. It has high specific power (power/weight ratio) and a high power density (power/volume ratio). It can also operate over a wide range of rotational speeds. Much of the traditional unreliability has been eradicated by the use of modern ignition systems and by fuel injection.

Despite over a century of development, major improvements in spark ignition engines have been taking place in the last decade. These have led to an increase in efficiency and a reduction in harmful emissions.

4.2.1 Efficiency of the spark ignition engine

Spark ignition engines work on a cycle that corresponds quite closely to the Otto cycle, in which heat is added rapidly, under constant volume conditions, just after the piston has reached top dead centre. The thermodynamic efficiency η of the Otto cycle is dependent on the volume compression ratio (R_v), and is given (see for example Agnew [4.1]) by

$$\eta = 1 - \frac{1}{R_v^{n-1}}$$

where n is the polytropic exponent. For operation in an ideal gas, n becomes γ, the ratio of the principal specific heats, which has the value of 1.4 for air. In practice a value of nearer 1.3 is appropriate for petrol/air mixtures.

In the spark ignition engine the maximum ratio that can be used is limited by the properties of the fuel. If the compression ratio is too high, the mixture will spontaneously combust or 'knock' before reaching the optimum point on the compression stroke, and this leads to excessive mechanical loading and reduced efficiency. In practice, however, it is not really the knock resistance of the fuel (expressed in terms of its octane rating) that nowadays limits the compression ratios used, but the fact that above a ratio of about 10:1 the mechanical friction rises, and gains in overall efficiency become insignificant. For road-going vehicles, compression ratios in the range of 9 to 10 are normally used.

Weakening the fuel/air mixture ratio improves the efficiency, albeit at the expense of a reduced specific power. Unfortunately, the chemical reactions involved and the high temperatures needed in the catalytic conversion process militate against the use of radical lean-burn technology, and the full potential for spark ignition engines cannot currently be realised. Efficiencies in the region of around 30% to 40% are currently attainable, but with suitable developments it is theoretically possible to push this significantly higher. The move to higher voltage electrical systems in cars allows the option of using electrically operated valves, which opens up many avenues for improvement in efficiency. In particular, at part load, it becomes possible to control the air flow by means of variable valve control rather than by the wasteful process of throttling.

4.2.2 Fuels and emissions

Spark ignition engines can be run on a range of liquid and gaseous fuels, including ethanol, methanol, liquefied petroleum gas (LPG), compressed natural gas (CNG) and even hydrogen, but the range is not as wide as that available for diesel engines. Noxious emissions, particularly carbon monoxide (CO), oxides of nitrogen (NOx) and sulphur dioxide (SOx) have been greatly reduced by improved combustion, and by the introduction of catalytic converters. SOx emissions are being lowered further by the introduction of low sulphur fuel. Improved combustion has also reduced CO output dramatically, particularly in the case of newer GDI (Gasoline Direct Injection) engines. Despite these advances, spark ignition engines still produce high levels of noxious emissions when cold, because the catalytic converters have to be heated to a high temperature to operate effectively. The majority of car journeys are short, and therefore taken with engines that are not fully warmed.

4.2.3 Advantages of the spark ignition engine for hybrid vehicle propulsion

The major attractions of the spark ignition engine are its high specific power (power/weight ratio), the rate at which it can be accelerated, and the range of rotational speeds over which it can be operated effectively. For a mild hybrid domestic car with a parallel configuration, the spark ignition engine is still, therefore, one of the most obvious choices. The two first-generation vehicles of this type, the Prius and the Insight, employ spark ignition engines.

Hybrid arrangements generally permit the spark ignition engine to be run at the most efficient operating conditions of speed and load. Figure 4.1 shows contours of constant engine efficiency (energy output/energy available in the fuel consumed) for varying speed and power output for a typical spark ignition engine.

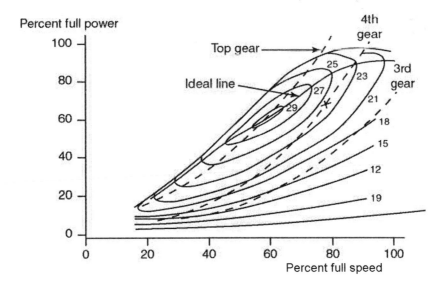

Figure 4.1: The variation of engine efficiency with speed and power for a typical spark ignition engine.

In figure 4.1, curves are also shown for the variation of power output with road speed for three gear ratios. The highest gear ratio allows the engine to be run at close to its maximum efficiency. For most vehicles with manual gearboxes, however, it is necessary to use a lower ratio than ideal, because there is insufficient reserve of power to allow reasonable acceleration without changing gear. A continuously variable transmission (CVT) system would enable the engine to be operated on the ideal line (the optimum driving locus) shown on the diagram; the gear ratio can be rapidly adjusted to suit the load conditions. Unfortunately, available mechanical CVT gearboxes have a lower efficiency than either a conventional manual shift gearbox, or even an automatic with lock-up on the top ratio. Until recently they also had a reputation for poor reliability and overhaul life.

In a series hybrid propulsion system, as with the CVT, there is no fixed relationship between the car speed and the engine speed. In addition, the engine output power does not even have to match the propulsion power demand in the short term, as the storage system can either make-up the shortfall if there is one, or absorb the excess. It is therefore possible to keep the engine operating at close to its maximum efficiency. In general, it will of course be necessary to vary the engine load to prevent the storage device becoming either over or under charged, but the range of operating conditions will generally be less than that required even with the CVT. The same effect can be obtained even on a parallel hybrid if a degree of effective CVT operation is available, as on the Prius.

Even with a pure parallel arrangement, the hybrid still enables the engine to be run at high efficiency. It will be seen from figure 4.1, that at low and high power output, the efficiency of the engine will be low, regardless of the gearing used. High power output is rarely used, but under steady low speed driving, the power requirement is often very low. In a hybrid vehicle, a smaller engine is used, which therefore has to operate at a higher percentage of its maximum power, and thus at a higher efficiency. The occasional demands for high power can be met using the stored energy device and its associated motor. Also, as with the series hybrid, when the requirement for propulsive power is low, excess engine power may be used to top up the storage device.

A further strong argument for the use of hybrid propulsion systems will be provided by the proposed move towards using 36/42 volt electrical systems on road vehicles. This move is being brought about in order to provide high-power electrical systems such as electrical power steering and even electrical valve lifting, without the need for bulky actuators and heavy cabling. The higher voltage will also permit rapid and smooth engine starting and restarting using powerful starter/generator units. This development will require the installation of larger capacity high-current batteries and higher-power alternator systems. With such systems installed, it will be almost pointless not to exploit them to produce at least a limited degree of hybrid propulsion.

4.3 The diesel engine

The first large-scale use of diesel engines dates from the period around 1923 to 1924 when the German manufacturers Benz, Daimler and MAN introduced diesel-engined trucks. Nowadays diesel engines are used for most commercial vehicles and buses, and their use in domestic cars is increasing.

4.3.1 Efficiency

Modern high speed diesel engines work on a cycle that is not very much different from the Otto cycle used in spark ignition engines, although the burning of the fuel lasts for a little longer than in the spark ignition engine, where combustion is almost instantaneous. In a diesel engine, the fuel is injected into the cylinders, rather than upstream at a carefully timed point in the cycle. Diesel engines operate at much higher compression ratios than spark ignition engines, and the efficiency is therefore inherently greater. Compression ratios of between 20 and 24 are commonly used, which is at least twice that used on spark ignition engines. This increases the theoretically realizable efficiency, which is further increased because air, rather than an air/fuel mixture, is compressed and also because the engine can run on a weak fuel/air ratio. Efficiencies as high as 48% can be obtained.

The relatively high efficiency makes the diesel engine an attractive option for commercial use, but because of the noise, vibration, harshness, smell and weight of the diesel engine it was considered unsuitable for domestic cars for many years. Technological developments have led to ever improving efficiency, and considerable progress has been made in reducing the noise and harshness, so that nowadays, diesel engines are becoming increasingly popular for cars.

A particular characteristic of the diesel is that it retains a reasonably high efficiency at part load, and diesel-engined vehicles are thus particularly suitable for urban use.

4.3.2 Diesel engine specific power and power density

Diesel engines produce less power from each cycle than a spark ignition engine of the same capacity (the power density is lower). The maximum rotational speed was for a long time limited by the mechanical injection systems used, and this also reduced the maximum power output. However, a 'common rail' high pressure fuel supply coupled with electrically operated injectors has largely removed this limitation, and the maximum rotational speed of modern diesel car engines is now comparable to that of spark ignition petrol (gasoline) engines.

Diesel engines characteristically tend to suffer from a form of harshness known as 'diesel knock', which is due to a sudden rapid rise in pressure that happens as soon as the spontaneous pressure-induced ignition starts. The result is more noise, and higher vibration levels than on a spark ignition engine. It should be noted, however, that these deficiencies are far less noticeable on modern designs.

The high mechanical stresses imposed by the knock, and high maximum pressure, mean that diesel engines have to be more robust and heavier than a spark ignition unit. Traditionally, diesel engines also used a heavier flywheel in order to damp the fluctuation in crankshaft speed, and this contributed to the poor acceleration. The greater weight and lower power density means that the diesel engine has a lower specific power (power/weight ratio) than a spark ignition engine.

The specific power can be significantly increased by use of a turbocharger, which can also improve the efficiency and reduce the harshness. The high efficiency has always been an attractive feature for commercial operation, and diesel propulsion has been used for the majority of trucks and buses for many years.

4.3.3 Fuels and emissions in diesel engines

An important feature of the diesel engine is that it can be run on a variety of fuels, including renewable energy sources such as vegetable oils and alcohols. There is increasing concern, however, over the hazards to health of the exhaust emissions, partly caused by incomplete combustion of the fuel. In particular, these include oxides of nitrogen (NOx), produced by high temperature combustion in air, oxides of sulphur (SOx), due to the sulphur content of the fuel, volatile organic compounds, due to incomplete combustion of the fuel, and particulate matter, a product of combustion. Of these, the finer particulate matter is considered particularly hazardous: comparable with smoking. This matter comprises carbon particles impregnated with potentially harmful organic compounds. Particulate matter is defined by its size. PM_{10} emission refers to particles around 10 microns in size while $PM_{2.5}$ refers to a size of 2.5 microns. Whilst the latter are less visible, they are considered more hazardous. There is concern that petrol (gasoline) engines also emit $PM_{2.5}$. These health hazards are the driving force behind the emissions legislation being gradually implemented, as described earlier.

Emissions of carbon monoxide and unburned hydrocarbons are generally lower than from spark ignition engines, and the problem of high emissions when cold is not nearly so marked for the diesel engine. This makes the diesel a better choice where the vehicle is to be used predominantly for short journeys. A great deal of effort has gone into the production of new low-emission fuels. By lowering the sulphur content of the fuel, the SOx can be reduced significantly. Low sulphur fuel is now widely available. NOx emissions remain more of a problem.

The greatest current disadvantage of the diesel lies in its tendency to produce significant amounts of particulates. The smaller sizes are difficult to trap or filter effectively. Improved injection and combustion control has led to significant reductions in particulate production, and there are some promising new approaches to particulate emission reduction, such as the use of ionisation of the exhaust gases, as described in Chapter 1. The particulate problem is currently the major obstacle to increased use of diesel engines, and it is not clear whether they will be able to meet the EURO IV limits. It should be noted, however, that particulate emissions can be low if the engine is operated at a near constant power setting, so particulate emissions should be much less of a problem with hybrid propulsion.

4.3.4 Advantages of diesel engines for hybrid vehicles

The problem of the poor acceleration of the diesel engine is largely solved in hybrid propulsion systems, because it is possible with some arrangements to keep the prime mover running at an almost constant speed and power. This is particularly the case with hybrid systems operating in series mode with a largely electrical transmission system.

The high efficiency, and the fact that automotive diesel engine technology is highly developed, makes these engines a popular choice for hybrid vehicles of all types, from small cars to trains. The demands of legislation requiring reduced CO_2 output are encouraging a rapid increase in the proportion of diesel-engined domestic cars.

For the series hybrid vehicle with electrical transmission there is the option of using a diesel generator set optimised in speed and power to give high efficiency and minimum emissions. Suitable generator sets based on diesel and spark ignition engines are currently under development for automotive applications.

4.4 Gas turbines

During the Second World War, the Rover Car Company was given the task of developing Whittle's aircraft gas turbine engine for production. This apparently strange choice of company was due to the fact that the aircraft engine manufacturers were heavily committed to the production and development of piston engines. After slow progress and bitter wrangling, the job was subsequently transferred to the Rolls-Royce aircraft engine company. Rover was, however, convinced that its technical knowledge could be exploited in producing gas turbines for automotive use in the post-war period. Unfortunately, despite much development work and considerable expenditure during the 1950s, the outcomes are now to be seen only in the museum at Gaydon.

Many of the features of the gas turbine that make these engines unsuitable for conventional vehicles, such as slow response rate and poor part-load efficiency, do not apply in the case of hybrids, so there has been renewed interest. A project featuring a gas turbine powered hybrid rail vehicle is described below.

4.4.1 Gas turbine efficiency

The gas turbine works on a cycle corresponding closely to the Brayton cycle, where heat is added and rejected at constant pressures. The efficiency is dependent on the pressure ratio between the inlet and the combustion chamber. Combustion takes place at a virtually constant pressure. Conventional current gas turbines have low efficiencies ranging between 15% and 30% depending on the degree of sophistication and the size, and whether a waste heat recuperator is incorporated. To approach anything like the efficiency of a spark ignition engine, the pressure ratio would need to be raised considerably above current values. Unfortunately raising the combustion pressure also raises its temperature, and at the very high ratios needed for efficiencies approaching 40%, it would be necessary to use ceramic components. Experimental engines with such components have been built, but there are doubts about the cost and practicability of these developments for automotive use.

   In addition to high-pressure ratios, high efficiency can only be realised if some of the waste heat in the exhaust can be captured and fed back into the system at the appropriate point. This means that a large regenerative heat exchanger has to be included, and this greatly increases the size, complexity and cost. This may rule out the gas turbine for small vehicles but they are being evaluated for buses and rail vehicles and are already used to power main-line express trains, principally in the USA and Egypt.

4.4.2 Gas turbine emissions

Gas turbines run on a weak fuel/air ratio, and tend to have low emissions of carbon monoxide and unburned hydrocarbons. NOx emissions are lower than those of reciprocating engines, and various techniques for NOx reduction are being developed. Like the diesel, gas turbines can be run on a wide range of fuels including hydrogen (the world's first successful gas turbine, built by von Ohain, ran initially on hydrogen). The inherently low level of noxious emissions is one of the main attractions of the gas turbine.

4.4.3 Specific power and power density of gas turbines

The power to weight ratio of the aeronautical gas turbine is very high, but some of this advantage is lost when the recuperator necessary for high efficiency is added. The recuperator also results in a bulky unit with a relatively poor power density. Again, this is more easily accommodated in larger vehicles.

4.4.4 Advantages of gas turbines for hybrid vehicles

Despite the relatively poor efficiency, the simplicity, reliability, low maintenance costs and low emissions make the gas turbine an attractive proposition for rail and heavy commercial vehicles.

For conventional automotive applications, there are a number of drawbacks to the gas turbine. The primary shaft will only operate over a small speed range, and the acceleration is poor, with a noticeable lag. Adding a second lower speed output shaft reduces the effect somewhat, but does not overcome it. For a hybrid vehicle, these problems are largely avoided, because the engine can be run at a near constant speed and power output. This is particularly the case with series hybrid vehicles.

Another problem for conventional vehicles is that the turbine shaft runs at very high speeds: at least ten times as fast as a spark ignition engine. Even with a twin shaft arrangement considerable step-down gearing is required, and high-speed gearboxes tend to be bulky and expensive. In a series hybrid where the transmission system is essentially electric, this problem is largely avoided. The main difficulty lies in the design of a generator unit that will withstand the dynamic forces associated with the very high rotational speeds. In the European ULEV-TAP project described by Etemad [4.2] this has presented a larger problem than had been anticipated. In this project, a 50 kW compact high-speed gas turbine generator set is being evaluated as prime mover in a hybrid flywheel system for a 30t light rail vehicle. The vehicle, illustrated in figure 4.2, uses a converted electrical tram, and employs a flywheel for energy storage. The flywheel is rated at 300 kW, which is easily sufficient for maximum traction power and for regenerative braking. Only around 50 kW was needed for the prime mover power. The traction motors are rated at 220 kW. The large difference between mean and maximum power demonstrates how the hybrid arrangement can utilise a much smaller prime mover than a conventional vehicle. Further details of this project are given in Chapter 7.

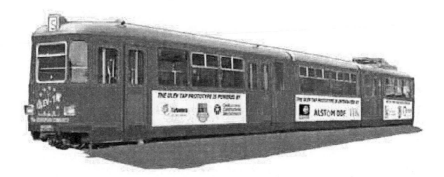

Figure 4.2:   Experimental hybrid tram designed for use with a gas turbine prime mover, as part of the European ULEV-TAP project [4.2].

Compact gas turbine generator sets with directly coupled permanent alternators have been developed in the UK and USA. These were originally developed for small combined heat and power applications, but are now considered a serious option as prime movers for hybrid electric vehicles. The high cost of this option relative to the diesel engine is potentially offset by the lower maintenance cost, due to the engine having only one major moving part.

There is intense competition at present between gas turbine development, mainly in the USA, and internal combustion engine development, mainly in Europe. The gas turbine has many attractive features as the basis for the volume production of compact, low-cost, high-efficiency prime mover units.

4.5 Stirling engines

Stirling cycle engines are designed to run on a cycle that corresponds closely to the reversible Carnot cycle, which gives the highest possible theoretical efficiency for given temperature limits. This cycle of operation involves adding heat to the working fluid at constant temperature during an isothermal expansion, which is followed by an adiabatic expansion. Heat is then rejected during an isothermal compression, which is followed by an adiabatic compression. Although it might be possible to build an internal combustion Stirling engine, practical engines built thus far have used external combustion, with the heat being applied to, and rejected from, the working fluid via heat exchangers. The working fluid can be air, but in advanced engines, hydrogen or helium are normally employed as the working fluid.

4.5.1 Stirling engine efficiency

The ideal efficiency of the Stirling engine is given by

$$\eta = 1 - \frac{T_{\min}}{T_{\max}}$$

The temperatures in this expression must be absolute values (degrees Kelvin). It will be seen from this, that if the minimum temperature reached is around standard ambient of 15°C (which corresponds to 288 K absolute), then for an efficiency of 50%, the maximum temperature must be 303°C (576 K). Thus, achieving a high efficiency requires the use of a heat exchanger radiator that runs at a very high temperature. Practical Stirling cycle engines are normally designed to run on hydrogen or helium as the working gas. This cannot be simply rejected and replaced by ambient temperature fluid at the start of each cycle, so the fluid has to be cooled in a heat exchanger, and it is difficult to cool this down to anything like ambient temperature. As may be inferred from the efficiency expression above, any increase in the minimum temperature makes it necessary to raise the maximum temperature even further to maintain the same ratio and efficiency.

One interesting possibility is to use a Stirling engine to convert waste heat from a gas turbine electrical generator set in a combined cycle arrangement. This could raise the overall efficiency significantly.

4.5.2 Stirling engine fuels and emissions

The Stirling engine normally works using external combustion with a heater and heat exchanger. It is possible to run the engine on almost anything that will burn, including farmyard waste. It is also relatively easy with external combustion to minimise the production of noxious gases. Carbon-based fuels will of course produce carbon dioxide, but due to the high efficiency, it will be proportionally less than for a petrol (gasoline) or even a diesel engine.

4.5.3 Specific power and power density of the Stirling engine

For a given cylinder swept volume, the amount of power that can be extracted from a cycle is much smaller than for the Otto cycle approximation of the spark ignition engine, so the Stirling engine has to be correspondingly larger. External combustion and a large high-temperature radiator also mean that the units are bulky. The power/weight ratio or specific power will depend on the form of construction used, and although experimental automotive Stirling engines have been built, the technology is not yet mature enough to enable a reliable estimate to be made of the potential specific power of fully developed engines.

4.5.4 Use of Stirling engines in hybrid vehicles

Several attempts have been made to develop automotive Stirling engines. Collie [4.3] describes two experimental series Stirling-electric hybrids Stir-Lec I and Stir-Lec II, built by General Motors in 1968 and 1969. Emissions of NOx were about half that produced by an Opel Kadett of the same period, and hydrocarbon emissions were negligible. GM did not, however, consider the vehicle to be commercially viable because of its cost and complexity, and the project was abandoned.

Poulton [4.4] describes an evaluation of a 58 kW Stirling engine in a non-hybrid test car in the early 1980s. Emissions were evaluated for the FTP cycle and gave HC at 0.14 g/km, CO at 1.19 g/km and NOx at 0.3 g/km. Apart from the NOx value, these figures comply with the EURO III requirements for petrol-engined cars. Lia and Schröder [4.5] describe a Stirling-electric hybrid concept being developed at the University of Lund in Sweden in the early 1990s.

A problem with Stirling engines has always been their large size and mass, and thus far, the use of Stirling engines has been almost entirely restricted to static applications. Because of the external combustion arrangements, initial start-up is slow. This factor coupled with the poor power density means that Stirling engines are unlikely to be used in conventional vehicles. However, in a hybrid, where the maximum output required is much lower, the engine can be smaller, and the potentially high efficiency of the Stirling engine makes it worthy of consideration. In public service vehicles including trains, start-up is not a significant problem, because the vehicles, once started, are normally left running for the whole day. City centre buses and trams often operate with a very low *average* power, and in a series hybrid vehicle this could be supplied efficiently by a small Stirling engine. The low emissions and the ability to run on unconventional fuels make these engines attractive in terms of environmental considerations. However, further development of the Stirling engine is currently being inhibited by the fact that fuel cells are seen as the more promising new technology.

4.6 Steam and other Rankine cycle engines

The most common form of Rankine vapour-power cycle engine is the steam engine. Similar types of engine running on fluids other than steam exist, but are normally found only in highly specialised applications such as in nuclear submarines; water is an extremely cheap and safe working fluid.

Steam engines were used for automotive applications for much longer than is generally thought. According to Faith [4.6], Sentinel steam trucks were still being exported from Great Britain to South America as late as the 1950s. The advantages for automotive use in the early days of motoring were quiet operation, high torque at low speed, and the fact that neither clutch nor gearbox were necessary. Disadvantages were the long start-up time from cold, and the high rate of consumption of water.

4.6.1 Rankine cycle engine efficiency

The efficiency of steam engines is inherently low, with a maximum of little more than 30%. Power stations can achieve a higher 'effective' efficiency by using the waste heat for other purposes such as providing heating to buildings. Very little else can be done to improve the efficiency significantly. There is, however, the possibility of using such an engine to convert waste heat from a gas turbine generator set in a combined cycle arrangement. This could raise the overall efficiency of the combination to an acceptable level. In this arrangement, and a similar alternative using the Stirling engine, one could have a series/parallel arrangement, with the gas turbine power transmitted electrically, and the Stirling or steam engine power transmitted mechanically (with high transmission efficiency). As far as is known, no such schemes are even at the drawing-board stage yet.

4.6.2 Rankine cycle engine fuels and emissions

Like the Stirling engine, the steam engine employs external combustion, and can be run on a wide variety of fuels. This includes hydrogen, which does not produce the greenhouse gas carbon dioxide. Whatever fuel is employed, external combustion means that the combustion process can be carefully controlled to minimise noxious emissions. A certain amount of energy storage and load levelling is inherent in the external combustion system, by virtue of the energy stored in the steam producer unit.

4.6.3 Rankine cycle engine specific power and power density

Automotive steam engines reached a high level of sophistication in the mid 20th century, and were nothing like the huge heavy and clumsy monsters used in rail transport. With oil firing, and compact flash boilers, the basic engine need not have a much higher specific power than the corresponding internal combustion engine. Nowadays, steam engines would be required to condense and re-use the water vapour in a closed cycle, and this would require a large condenser. Steam engines therefore have a relatively poor power/volume ratio or power density, which makes them unattractive for automotive applications.

4.6.4 Use of Rankine cycle engines in hybrid vehicles

The hybrid configuration makes the use of these alternative prime movers a realistic possibility, as the problem of rapid response to driver demand actions is overcome. As with the Stirling engine, the external combustion allows a careful control of emissions, and the slow start up from cold would not be a problem for rail transport or heavy haulage. Even in a domestic car, the stored energy would allow the vehicle to be driven off before the combustion system had reached operating temperature. The wide range of suitable fuels may also show environmental advantages. In economic terms, the ability to run on cheap fuels might offset the low efficiency. The environmental impact of using carbon-based fuels at a low efficiency would, however, probably exclude serious consideration of the Rankine engine in comparison with other competing alternatives.

4.7 Fuel cells

Fuel cells provide a means of producing electrical energy directly by reacting hydrogen and oxygen. The only direct by-product is water. As the energy conversion efficiency is high, fuel cells are seen as an extremely promising form of automotive power unit for the future. The proposed commercial introduction, however, keeps being delayed due to a number of technical and infrastructure problems.

There is a strong body of opinion that fuel cell vehicles will need to be of hybrid form, with batteries being used for initial power during warm up, and for smoothing out the short-term demands of power supply and brake energy recovery. It has to be admitted, however, that this view is not universally held, and both General Motors and Daimler-Chrysler have at one time expressed a wish to avoid the hybrid approach.

The process of converting hydrogen and oxygen into water and electricity is effectively electrolysis of water in reverse. However, reversing the process requires a means of recombining hydrogen and oxygen and there are two fundamental ways of achieving this, namely using a proton exchange membrane (PEM) or using an alkaline electrolyte.

4.7.1 The proton exchange membrane fuel cell

In the first type, the core element is normally a solid polymer electrolyte bounded by platinum layers forming the anode and cathode. At the anode, hydrogen is absorbed into the electrolyte as hydrogen ions or protons, having given up their electron to the anode, which forms the negative output of the cell. The membrane is designed so that only the protons can pass through to the cathode, where they combine with oxygen and an electron to form water, which is drawn off. The process causes the cathode to become positively charged relative to the anode. To complete the circuit, electrons flow from the anode to the cathode via the external load, driven by the potential difference. Externally, therefore, the fuel cell has the characteristics of a battery cell. The difference is that provided the hydrogen and air flow continuously, then so will the electric current. The chemical processes at the electrodes can be expressed thus:

Anode $\qquad$ $H_2 \quad \rightarrow \quad 2H^+ + 2e^-$ $\qquad$ (e = electron)

Cathode $\qquad$ $\tfrac{1}{2}O_2 + 2H^+ + 2e^- \quad \rightarrow \quad H_2O$

A schematic of the PEM fuel cell operation is shown in figure 4.3. The membrane comprises an electrolyte, which can be of various types. Solid polymer, solid oxide, phosphoric acid and molten carbonate are examples of electrolytes used in current developments. The membrane is designed to keep the hydrogen and oxygen separate, whilst allowing the passage of protons (H^+) through to the cathode to react with the incoming oxygen.

4.7.2 Disadvantages of the PEM

Because of the acidic environment, the PEM fuel cell requires a platinum catalyst to engender the reaction between the protons and the oxygen. This adds to the cost of the fuel cell, which is likely to be aggravated by the limited worldwide availability of platinum if PEM fuel cells are ever mass-produced for the automotive market. This would push up the price of platinum and PEM technology, unless a more abundant alternative can be found.

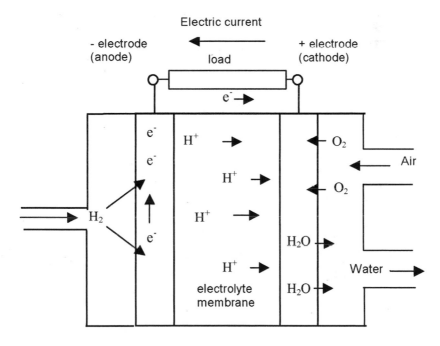

Figure 4.3: Schematic of proton exchange membrane fuel cell.

4.7.3 The alkaline fuel cell

This is an alternative form of fuel cell involving a different reaction. The use of an alkaline electrolyte allows alternatives to platinum to be used as a catalyst. In an alkaline fuel cell, hydrogen reacts with the electrolyte, normally potassium hydroxide solution, through a porous negatively charged anode. In the presence of a catalyst, hydrogen atoms yield their electrons to the anode to form positively charged hydrogen ions (protons) that combine with hydroxide ions in the electrolyte to form water, half of which can be removed continuously. At the cathode, oxygen and the remaining water combine with electrons to form hydroxide ions, which diffuse back to the anode through the electrolyte.

Electrons flow from the anode to the cathode through the load, as in the PEM fuel cell. The reactions can be summarised thus:

Anode $H_2 + 2\,OH^- \rightarrow 2\,H_2O + 2e^-$ (e = electron)

Also $H_2 \rightarrow 2H^+ + 2e^-$ (as in PEM)

Cathode $\tfrac{1}{2}\,O_2 + 2H^+ + 2e^- \rightarrow H_2O$

               $H_2O + \tfrac{1}{2}\,O_2 + 2e^- \rightarrow 2\,OH^-$

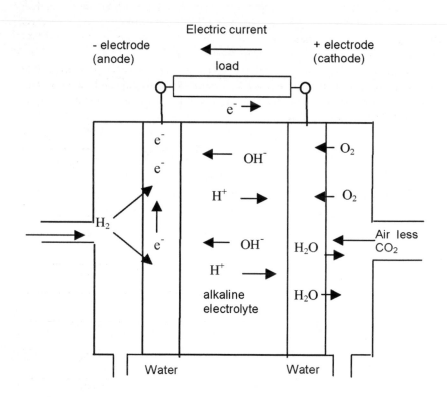

Figure 4.4:   Schematic of the alkaline fuel cell.

The reactions are assisted by the catalyst, and the alkaline electrolyte provides a medium by which the negative OH ions can migrate from anode to cathode. Electrons flow from cathode to anode via the load, so completing the circuit, and forming the electric current output, as in the PEM fuel cell.

In the alkaline fuel cell, CO_2 must be removed from the air, otherwise it reacts with the electrolyte. This is a fairly simple, but rather bulky process of passing the air through lime.

4.7.4 Conversion efficiency of fuel cells

Efficiencies of conversion from gaseous hydrogen and oxygen to electrical power output as high as 60% have been demonstrated for both PEM and alkaline fuel cells. Figure 4.5 shows the relative conversion efficiencies of various types of plant. Other fuel cell types are listed here, for comparison, but detailed description is beyond the scope of this book. It should be mentioned that the direct methanol fuel cell is of interest because of its ability to operate with methanol as a fuel, which is more practical than hydrogen, and more readily available. Apart from this, the PEM and alkaline fuel cells are presently leading contenders for automotive applications. Their relatively high conversion efficiency needs to be weighed against the large energy use associated with the production of hydrogen, since the overall system efficiency depends also on the

Source	Efficiency %
Alkaline fuel cell	55-60
Proton exchange membrane fuel cell	30-50
Direct methanol fuel cell	35-40
Phosphoric acid fuel cell	45-45
Molten carbonate fuel cell	50-60
Solid oxide fuel cell	50-55
1MW gas turbine (natural gas)	20-35
Automotive petrol (gasoline) engine generator	25

Figure 4.5:   Comparative efficiencies of electrical power sources.

efficiency of hydrogen production. It can, however, be argued that if the hydrogen is produced using renewable sources such as wind, wave, geothermal, solar or hydro power, both the cost and the environmental impact will be favourable. The use of hydrogen produced from renewable sources would also reduce the worldwide dependence on oil. If hydrogen is to be the fuel of the future, then the high efficiency of the fuel cell makes it the preferred option for vehicle propulsion.

4.7.5 Fuels for fuel cells

Gaseous hydrogen has a poor energy density at atmospheric pressure, so for automotive purposes it will probably need to be at high pressures. Compressed gaseous hydrogen storage has been adopted by Ford for its experimental fuel-cell powered Focus.

An alternative is to liquefy the hydrogen, but unfortunately, hydrogen liquefies at the very low temperature of $-253°C$, which is only $20°$ above absolute zero ($-273°C$). Daimler-Chrysler consider that storage at this temperature is a viable option, and General Motors has shown an 80 kW demonstration vehicle, HydroGen 1, with cryogenic liquid hydrogen stored in a twin-walled vacuum insulated steel tank. For vehicle fleet operation this approach may be acceptable, but for domestic use, there is the problem of what happens when the vehicle is (perhaps unintentionally) left for long periods of time so that the fuel starts to warm up and evaporate. Venting gaseous hydrogen safely is not easy. Cryogenic hydrogen is extremely dangerous, and must not be allowed to come into contact with humans. The potential effects of accidental spillage are almost too horrific to contemplate. Another major objection to the use of liquid hydrogen is that the liquefaction process takes some 30% of the available energy, so the overall system efficiency is low. Pure hydrogen has a high specific energy of 120 MJ/kg, which compares very favourably with petrol (gasoline) that is around 40 MJ/kg.

Another option is to store the hydrogen in the form of hydrides, but this is bulky, and there are problems of recharging. Nevertheless, this approach has been actively pursued by Toyota, and demonstrated in its FCHV3 vehicle. In the autumn of 2000, Energy Conversion Devices of Troy, Michigan announced that it had produced an advanced hydride storage system weighing 120 kg with a volume of 120 litres (about twice the size of a large car petrol (gasoline) tank) that would give a 500 km range [4.7].

Hydrogen can be extracted or 'reformed' from a number of different liquids, including alcohols (methanol and ethanol), ammonia, and various oil-derived hydrocarbons, including petrol (gasoline). General Motors has favoured the use of reformed gasoline. At first sight, there might appear to be little point in using petroleum or oil products, why not continue to use conventional petrol engines? The advantage of the fuel cell is its relatively high conversion efficiency, and the fact that energy is produced directly in the form of electricity, which is easy to transmit and control. The number of moving parts is also minimal.

Once a hydrogen reformer is added, the overall system becomes bulky. There can also be noxious by-products with some fuels. Methanol is a popular choice, as there is a worldwide glut of this fuel, which is very easy to produce. It has been championed by Daimler-Chrysler, but the fact that it burns with an almost invisible flame and is quite toxic, has deterred some manufacturers. The level of noxious emissions is such that it will not qualify under Californian rules as a ZEV (zero emissions vehicle).

The fact that different manufacturers are still arguing over which methods of hydrogen production and transport to use, indicates that it may take some time for the technology to develop and standardise.

4.7.6 Fuel cell emissions

When running on pure hydrogen and air, the by-products are almost entirely water vapour and harmless nitrogen. Due to the low temperature of operation (80°C), oxides of nitrogen are not formed. The water vapour could cause local environmental problems in areas such as the Los Angeles basin, which is already susceptible to natural mist and fog conditions. Water vapour can contribute to the greenhouse effect, and it may therefore be necessary to condense it. It should also be appreciated that in terms of reducing greenhouse gas emissions, conventional internal combustion engines can be run on hydrogen and produce mainly water as the by-product, although NOx emissions will be produced if air is used.

Ammonia can be reformed to produce hydrogen, and should similarly produce only nitrogen and water as by-products, but any accidental spillage or leakage of the raw fuel could be catastrophic. Hydrocarbon fuels will produce a number of unwanted by-products including complex organic compounds, which may be difficult to dispose of. They also produce carbon dioxide, thus rendering the fuel-cell vehicle less environmentally friendly, and carbon monoxide, which has to be treated to convert it to the more harmless carbon dioxide. Petroleum reformers work at high enough temperatures to cause the production of oxides of nitrogen.

4.7.7 Fuel cell specific power and power density

Recent advances in fuel cell design have drastically reduced the basic fuel cell unit to a size that can be accommodated easily in road vehicles, with power densities as high as 1.3 kW/litre, and a specific power of around 0.5 kW/kg. The fuel cell unit is therefore now comparable in size to an internal combustion engine of similar power output. The size increases considerably, however, if a fuel reformer is used, but several demonstration vehicles have now been produced with acceptable packaging of the power plant and fuel storage. These include the Mercedes Necar 4, based on the small A class Mercedes. If environmental considerations dominate, the large volume of a reformer and fuel cell propulsion unit may simply come to be regarded as a price that has to be paid. In some forms of operation such as rail transport, the volume of the power plant is not quite so critical as in a domestic car.

4.7.8 Fuel cell operating life and performance

The operating life of the main components of fuel cells is almost indefinite, although there are a number of mechanical parts such as pumps that would have a finite life. A slight degradation in power output with use (1% in 1000 hours) has been recorded. A battery can respond rapidly to changes in demand power, but this is not the case with a fuel cell, where reaction rates and consequently power output are controlled externally. This has been a disadvantage when batteries have been replaced by fuel cells in electric vehicles, since power output must respond instantly to driver needs. The main market for fuel cells to date has been in static local power generation and marine applications, where dynamic response is not so critical.

4.7.9 Suitability for hybrid propulsion

The fuel cell represents a promising prime mover for a series hybrid electric vehicle, as the efficiency is high, and the energy is provided directly in electrical form. The bulk of the fuel cell may be reduced in a hybrid system because the fuel cell only needs to be large enough to supply the average power requirements. The stored energy device can provide short-term boosts of power, and absorb the braking energy. The storage device can also be used for cold starting while the reformer reaches its running conditions. Fuel cell warm-up time is often cited as a major objection to the use of fuel cells in domestic cars, but developments such as those incorporated in the Honda FCX-V3 have reduced this to a matter of seconds rather than minutes. When a fuel reformer is used, however, the start-up time is considerably longer, since higher temperatures are involved. Demonstration vehicles using reformers generally employ a tank of pure hydrogen for start-up.

Fuel cell propulsion systems are currently quite complex, and it is understandable that Daimler-Chrysler and General Motors are reluctant at this stage to contemplate the added complication of hybrid propulsion. However, solving the problems of starting and transient loads without hybridisation, may end up in producing even more complexity. The demands of ever-higher energy efficiency will almost inevitably drive manufacturers to exploiting the advantages that can be obtained in terms of reduction in prime mover size and of regenerative braking. Fuel cell vehicles already have all the elements of electric propulsion, transmission and control in place, so adding a high output battery or ultracapacitor unit should not entail much additional complexity.

For several years, the large-scale introduction of the fuel cell as a means of automotive propulsion has been claimed to be imminent, but the anticipated date for large-scale introduction keeps slipping. Ballard have now developed fuel cells to a high level of practicality, and most of the major car producers have devoted a large amount of research and development effort to fuel cell propulsion. The problem of what fuel to use and how to store and distribute it remains a major obstacle. A further problem, as already mentioned, is that current fuel cells, in particular PEM fuel cells, use significant amounts of platinum, which is an extremely expensive and rare metal. Ballard have managed to reduce the amount used to less than half a gram per kilowatt of maximum power output, but this still amounts to some 40 grams for a typical vehicle power plant. There are also political implications, as the production of platinum is mostly controlled by the Russians and the South Africans. The rarity of the metal is also a major consideration, as there will probably not be enough of this material to supply the world's automotive industry. This explains the current interest in the development of the alkaline fuel cells, which allow the use of alternative catalysts. Finding an alternative is almost a prerequisite for the large-scale introduction of fuel cell vehicles, and considerable research and development effort is being directed to the problem.

4.8 Prime mover choices: summary and conclusions

All the prime movers described above have competing claims for their suitability in hybrid vehicles. The problem in making a choice is that they are all continually jockeying for position. Advances in diesel engine technology may give the diesel a temporary advantage but this may be quickly overtaken by corresponding progress in spark ignition engine design.

Fuel cell vehicles only offer an advantage in terms of greenhouse gases if the whole process, including the fuel production, reduces carbon dioxide emissions. Much of the perceived environmental advantage of the fuel cell comes from the fact that it operates on hydrogen, and thus produces only water as a by-product. However, spark ignition engines can also be run on hydrogen, and emissions of NOx can be reduced to very low levels by catalytic conversion. Gas turbines can similarly be run on hydrogen and have inherently low NOx emissions. The advantages of the fuel cell remain its freedom from vibration, low noise and absence of local harmful emissions. The fact that it produces electricity directly, makes it particularly attractive in series hybrid configurations.

Whatever prime mover is selected, a hybrid propulsion system should improve the efficiency, by allowing it to run at a more constant optimised speed and load. Diesel and spark ignition engines will probably continue to hold a dominant position for many years to come, and if the problem of particulate emissions can be overcome, the diesel may become the more popular due to its higher efficiency. Compact optimised diesel generator sets are already being developed for series hybrid electric vehicle applications.

4.9 References

[4.1]   Agnew, Brian, The design of engine characteristics for vehicle use, in *An Introduction to Modern Vehicle Design*, Ed. Julian Happian-Smith, Butterworth Heinemann, ISBN 0-7506-5044-3, Oxford, U.K., 2001, pp. 371-402.

[4.2]   Etemad, S. Ultra Low Emission Vehicle - Transport using advanced propulsion (ULEV-TAP), *Proc. 32nd ISATA Conference*, Vienna, June 1999, Paper 99CPE019, Automotive Automation Ltd, 42 Lloyd Pk Av, Croydon CR0 5SB, UK.

[4.3]   Collie, M. J. (editor), *Electric and Hybrid Vehicles*, Noyes Data Corp., New Jersey, USA, 1979.

[4.4]   Poulton, M. L., *Alternative Engines for Road Vehicles*, Computational Mechanics Publications, ISBN 1-85312-300-5, Southampton, 1994.

[4.5]   Lia, T. A. and Schröder, C., City Car 2007, Stirling-electric drive train for ultra low emission vehicles, *Proceedings of the Conference Next Generation Technologies for Efficient Energy End Uses and Fuel Switching,* International Energy Agency/Bundesministerium für Forschung und Technologie, Dortmund, Germany, 1992.

[4.6]   Faith, N., *Classic Trucks: Power on the Move*, Boxtree, ISBN 0-7522-1021-1, 1995.

[4.7]   Crosse, Jesse, A whole new business, *Automotive World*, November 2000, Automotive World Publications, London, pp. 38-43, 2000.

Chapter 5

PERFORMANCE: POWER AND ENERGY REQUIREMENTS

5.1 Types of hybrid vehicle and their performance criteria

As described in the first chapter, the generic term, hybrid vehicle, covers a wide range of possible configurations and specifications. At one end of the spectrum, the hybrid vehicle may be a BEV (battery electric vehicle) with extended range provided by a small internal combustion (i.c.) engine/generator set, which keeps the batteries at least partially topped up. At the other end of the spectrum are 'mild' hybrids or *mybrids* which are similar to traditional vehicles (road or rail) but which employ a relatively small amount of energy storage capacity, that can be used both as a sink for regenerative braking, and as a power source for a short duration performance boost. The performance criteria and methods of optimisation of hybrid vehicles will depend on their usage, and the level of energy storage provided.

5.1.1 The hybridised battery electric vehicle

The battery electric vehicle is normally intended for use in urban environments where very low or zero emissions are required. The performance capabilities of the hybrid version are similar to those of a pure electric vehicle, apart from the extended range and endurance that the engine top-up provides. At one time, it was thought that with this class of vehicle, battery charging from the electricity mains would normally supply much of the stored energy. However, although this provides zero emissions in the immediate locality, the advantages in terms of cost savings and overall global emissions are not clear-cut. The overall or 'well-to wheel' efficiency is inherently low due to the large number of intermediate stages involved. If the requirement is for low but non-zero vehicle emissions, it will often be advantageous to use an internal combustion engine of sufficient size to make the vehicle independent of external charging. This is particularly the case with applications such as urban buses, where the time-average power output is low. Even though the engine size may not necessarily be much smaller than that required for a conventional bus, the hybrid has the advantage that it can operate for moderate distances as a purely electric vehicle. This feature may become more important if parts of large cities become subjected to regulations requiring zero emissions.

5.1.2 The mild hybrid

The mild hybrid or mybrid is intended as a replacement for conventional vehicles, and simply exploits the advantages of the hybrid concept to reduce the fuel consumption with a consequential reduction in emissions. In general, the prime mover and the secondary power source can be used individually or together. The performance requirements will be similar to those of conventional vehicles. Long range, high speed and good acceleration are required. The energy storage requirements are quite modest, and the hybrid arrangement allows adequate performance to be obtained using a smaller internal combustion engine than would be required for a conventional vehicle. The Toyota Prius and Honda Insight cars described in Chapter 7 are considered to fall into this category, but there is no agreed precise definition of what constitutes a mybrid.

Figure 5.1 illustrates how the required amount of stored energy varies with the maximum available prime-mover power, for the case of a typical family saloon car.

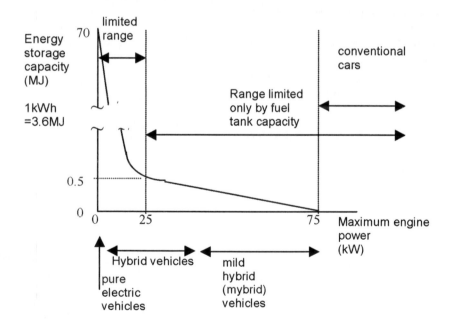

Figure 5.1:   Required energy storage capacity vs. required engine power for the case of a family saloon car.

The extreme left of the figure represents the case of a pure stored-energy vehicle such as a battery electric vehicle with no internal combustion engine.

With around 70 MJ of stored energy, the vehicle would have a range of about 80 km and a cruise speed of 110 km/h.

One reason for moving to a hybrid arrangement is to extend the range. Figure 5.1 illustrates the effect of fitting more and more powerful internal combustion engines (or other prime movers). The amount of stored energy required diminishes as the maximum power available from the prime mover is increased. Above a certain engine power (around 25 kW for a family sized car), the prime mover can supply sufficient power to meet the time-average power requirement of the vehicles, and the storage device simply acts to smooth out the demand. The vehicle range will be then be limited only by the capacity of the fuel tank, as in a conventional car. There is thus a straight trade-off between energy storage and maximum installed engine power. An increase in maximum engine power decreases the requirement for stored energy, and eliminates it altogether at around 75 kW which is the typical power required for a standard family saloon car with modest performance.

Towards the centre right-hand side of the diagram is the mild hybrid or mybrid category, where vehicles have most of the features of a conventional car but with the addition of some energy storage capacity.

Whatever type of hybrid is envisaged, the same basic expressions that determine the performance and efficiency will apply. However, the criteria for selecting the amount of energy storage will be a little different.

5.2 Tractive force, power and energy requirements

We will now focus on some of the basic considerations for sizing the energy storage and prime mover in hybrid vehicles.

5.2.1 Power

For vehicle propulsion, power is required for four primary purposes:

1   to provide acceleration
2   to enable the vehicle to ascend a gradient
3   to overcome aerodynamic resistance
4   to overcome rolling resistance

In addition, power is needed:

5   to overcome internal transmission and conversion losses
6   to accelerate the rotating components such as wheels, engine and transmission elements
7   to power auxiliaries, such as heating, ventilation and air conditioning.

It is sometimes convenient to separate out the power required to overcome *internal* losses from the vehicle *output* power. The first four items taken together represent the vehicle output power: the power that must be applied through the driven wheels at the road or rail interface (P_r). The power output from the motors (P_m) has to be significantly greater than this to accommodate items 5, 6 and 7.

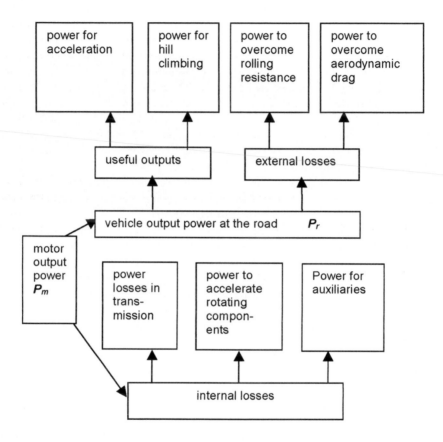

Figure 5.2: The power requirements of a vehicle.

5.2.2 Acceleration and hill climbing

The power required for a steady rate of acceleration is the product of the mass m, the acceleration a, and the speed V:

$$P = m\, a\, V. \tag{5.1}$$

The power required for climbing a hill inclined at an angle θ to the horizontal at a steady speed is the product of the weight component ($W \sin \theta$) and the speed:

$$P = (W \sin \theta)\, V. \tag{5.2}$$

5.2.3 Wheel rolling resistance

The wheel rolling resistance force (F_r) depends directly on the normal reaction between the vehicle and the road or track, and a factor known as the rolling resistance coefficient (k_r), which in turn depends primarily on the material properties of the tyre. On a level road, the normal reaction is the weight less any aerodynamic lift. Most road vehicles other than racing cars are nowadays designed to produce very little lift, so the influence of lift can normally be neglected. The rolling resistance force is then given simply by

$$F_r = W \, k_r . \tag{5.3}$$

As a first approximation, k_r is often taken as constant, with a value of around 0.012 for car tyres. In reality the coefficient is a rather complicated function of speed, temperature, tyre pressure and surface properties, but up to around 130 km/h the changes can be neglected for most practical purposes. Figure 5.3 shows the typical variation of the factor with road speed. Special low-loss tyres have been demonstrated, but as these give poorer adhesion, they have not been widely adopted. Rail vehicles have a much lower rolling resistance coefficient of around 0.0005 to 0.002, which largely accounts for the high energy efficiency of rail transport.

(Note that since the rolling resistance is proportional to the *normal* reaction force, there will be a slight reduction in this force when the vehicle is on a hill. In practical terms, however, this reduction is negligible.)

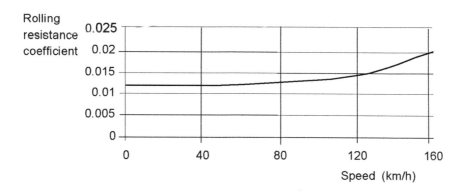

Figure 5.3: The variation of rolling resistance coefficient with vehicle speed.

The power required to overcome the rolling resistance is simply given by the product of the resistance force and the vehicle speed V:

$$P = (W \, k_r) \, V. \tag{5.4}$$

5.2.4 Aerodynamic drag

In still air, for a given vehicle speed V and air density ρ, the aerodynamic drag D depends on the product of the projected frontal area A and the drag coefficient C_D:

$$D = \frac{1}{2} \rho V^2 A C_D .\qquad(5.5)$$

The frontal area is dictated largely by packaging constraints, so drag reduction requires that the drag coefficient C_D should be as low as possible.

The drag coefficient depends on the shape of the vehicle, and in recent decades, a considerable amount of research has been directed at minimising the drag coefficient of all types of vehicles from domestic and racing cars to heavy commercial vehicles, as described by Barnard [5.1] and Hucho [5.2]. Figure 5.4 illustrates the progress that has been made as a result.

Type of vehicle	Pre-1970	Current	Probable near future
Domestic cars	0.4 - 0.55	0.25 - 0.35	0.2 - 0.35
Light vans	0.4 - 0.6	0.3 - 0.4	0.28 - 0.35
Buses	0.5 - 0.9	0.4 - 0.7	0.3 - 0.5
Articulated trucks	0.7 - 0.95	0.55 - 0.8	0.5 - 0.7

Figure 5.4:   Trends in the drag coefficient for various types of vehicle. The figures given are only a guide, and do not include extreme cases. The wide range predicted for domestic cars reflects the fact that style may often override other considerations.

The drag coefficient C_D for production domestic cars is nowadays normally in the range 0.25 to 0.35, although the lower value is rather exceptional. It should be noted, however, that these values of C_D only apply to vehicles moving in still air. In the presence of atmospheric wind, the drag will vary with the relative wind direction. This problem can be dealt with by using a 'wind corrected' drag coefficient, which takes account of the average relative wind velocity, as outlined by Buckley *et al.* [5.3]. For the purposes of comparisons between hybrid and conventional vehicles, however, these effects can be ignored.

As shown later, in hybrid vehicles, the achievement of a low drag coefficient is particularly important, as it largely determines the amount of continuously available power required for cruising. By contrast, in conventional vehicles, the maximum engine power required is primarily determined by the acceleration required.

The achievement of very low drag coefficients imposes considerable constraints on the styling, which is a major factor in the marketing of domestic vehicles. The Honda Insight hybrid shown in figure 5.5 achieves a creditable C_D of 0.25 within an acceptable styling and production engineering package. As described in reference [5.1], the styling requirements for low drag vary according to the type of vehicle. In cars, most of the drag is associated with the pressure distribution around the vehicle. As long as the front is reasonably well rounded, it is the rear end shape that has the major influence. The pronounced rear-end taper, which may be seen on the Honda Insight (figure 5.5), is generally conducive to low drag. With large commercial vehicles and buses, a significant contribution comes from surface friction drag on the sides, top and underbody. As long as these surfaces do not have significant gaps, protrusions or discontinuities, and the front end of the vehicle is well rounded at its front corners, the drag coefficient can be as low as 0.3.

Figure 5.5:   The Honda Insight hybrid, which shows a high degree of rear-end taper aimed at producing low drag.

On rail vehicles, surface friction drag may be the major contribution because of the relatively large ratio of side area to frontal area. For low drag rail vehicles, it is thus necessary to minimise discontinuities on the sides, top and underside. This involves flush-fitting doors and windows, with the gaps between carriages being reduced by means of flexible seals. Because of the importance of surface friction effects in train drag, the drag coefficient is highly dependent on the train length. An express train may typically have a drag coefficient in the order of 2.5.

Figure 5.6: Modern high-speed trains have a well-rounded and usually raked front.

As with all types of vehicle, the drag due to the front-end shape can be minimised quite easily by having a well-rounded form as in figure 5.6.

The power required to overcome aerodynamic drag is simply the product of the drag and the vehicle speed V, thus

$$P = \frac{1}{2} \rho V^3 A C_D \,. \tag{5.6}$$

The above terms may be combined to give the overall expression for the total motor output power required:

$$P_m = maV + (W \sin \theta)V + (W k_r)V + \frac{1}{2}\rho V^3 A C_D + [\text{internal losses}]$$
$$+ [\text{power to overcome internal inertia}] + [\text{power to auxiliaries}] \tag{5.7}$$

5.2.5 Internal losses and inertia

The determination of the internal power losses and the power required to accelerate the internal components can be quite complex. The various internal components will rotate at different speeds, and the relationship to the vehicle speed is not linear. Rotational speed changes can be stepped or variable according to the type of transmission used. Full performance calculations have to take account of the detailed characteristics of all the elements in the vehicle's drive train, and for this purpose, computer simulations are required, as described later.

The power required to overcome the internal rotational inertia represents a loss of energy in conventional vehicles, but in hybrid vehicles, a proportion of this may be recovered into the energy storage device. A significant proportion of the rotational energy is attributable to the wheels and final drive components, and as these are at the end of the drive chain, there are transmission losses associated with producing this rotational energy.

Simulations of vehicle performance require the modelling of dynamic characteristics of the internal components, and are thus strongly dependent on the configuration and detailed design of the individual vehicle.

5.2.6 Energy and stored energy capacity

The energy E required for a powered stage of a journey is given by summing or integrating the power over time

$$E = \int P \, dt \tag{5.8}$$

Some of this energy can be supplied by the main engine, but in a hybrid vehicle some can be released from a storage system to supplement the main engine power when required. During braking, the energy absorbed by the brakes is given by

$$E = \int F_b V \, dt \tag{5.9}$$

where F_b is the braking force at the road.

Optimisation of the amount of stored energy is a difficult balancing act. The storage device will have a mass, and will thus contribute to the overall mass of the vehicle. Increasing the total mass of the vehicle will increase the amount of power required to accelerate it or move it up a hill, so it is important not to provide a storage device that is larger than is strictly necessary. However, if the energy storage device is too small, the amount of braking energy that can be stored will be limited. Also, the prime mover will have to be large enough to provide a high proportion of the power during acceleration, so the potential advantage offered by the hybrid configuration will be diminished. Clearly, this optimisation process is strongly influenced by the *specific energy* of the storage device (stored energy/weight). With a high specific energy, the added mass penalty is relatively small. The *specific power* (power/weight ratio) of the storage unit also comes into the optimisation process, as the storage device has to be able to provide the energy at the necessary rate.

5.2.7 Spare capacity in energy storage

In addition to reducing the useful power output, transmission losses and the rotational inertia of internal components mean that not all of the stored energy will reach the driving wheels, so provision for this must be made in the storage capacity. The stored energy capacity must also be further increased to allow for the fact that in most types of storage device, it is usually impractical to fully drain the unit; indeed, in some types of battery, letting the charge level fall below 90% of full charge on a regular basis can cause a rapid deterioration in battery performance.

5.2.8   Basic elements involved in the modelling and simulation of hybrid vehicle performance

In order to design and evaluate hybrid propulsion systems, it is necessary to consider complete driving cycles. An example of an urban driving cycle is given in figure 5.7.

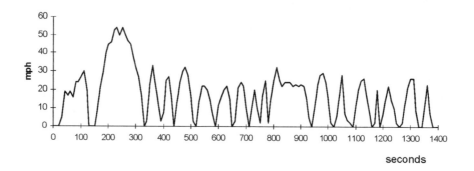

Figure 5.7: The US FTP75 urban drive cycle.

For a proper understanding of both the underlying physics and the mathematical analysis, it is useful to look at the performance requirements for each separate element of the cycle, namely: acceleration, cruise, deceleration and standstill. To an approximation, most urban drive cycles, including that shown in figure 5.7, can be considered as a sequence of such elemental cycles.

Figure 5.8(a) shows a speed/time diagram for one element of a drive cycle or a public transport vehicle. In this case, for passenger comfort, an initially uniform acceleration has been specified, followed by acceleration at constant power. The corresponding theoretical power demand on the propulsion system is shown in figure 5.8(b). For domestic cars, there is normally a short period of near constant acceleration dictated by tyre adhesion.

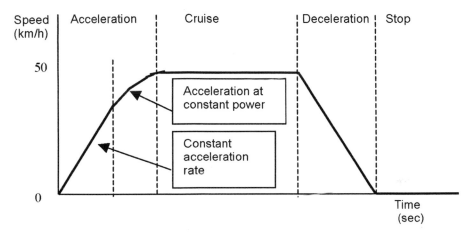

Figure 5.8(a): Simple idealised speed profile for a public transport vehicle start/stop cycle.

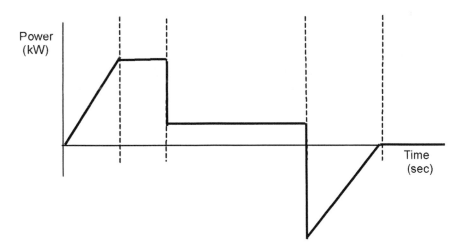

Figure 5.8(b): Corresponding power demand.

Vehicles with a continuously variable transmission (CVT) or with a sophisticated automatic transmission tend to accelerate at almost constant power after a short initial period at near constant acceleration. Manual transmission vehicles produce a complex acceleration curve due to the effects of gear changes. In the example shown in figure 5.8, the power rises steadily during the constant acceleration phase, after which it becomes limited by the engine power, producing a gradually reducing acceleration. At the end of the acceleration phase, the power demand falls immediately to a lower steady level for cruise at constant speed. During the deceleration phase, the power required is negative; that is, energy has to be either absorbed or dissipated. In a conventional vehicle, the energy is mostly dissipated in the braking system. Some energy is also dissipated by the pumping effect within the engine, and by the rolling and aerodynamic resistance. In an electrical or hybrid vehicle, much of the energy can be absorbed into the storage device by regenerative braking.

5.3 Performance factors in the various elements of the journey cycle

For illustrative purposes, we will consider as a case study, a mild hybrid car that is intended to produce a similar performance to that of a conventional medium sized European or Far Eastern vehicle. The basic data used are given in figure 5.9.

Mass with driver only	1300 kg
Fully laden mass	1800 kg
Rolling resistance coefficient	0.012
Projected frontal area	1.95 m^2
Transmission efficiency	90%
Drag coefficient C_D	0.3

Figure 5.9:   Data for a hypothetical medium sized domestic European car used as an example in the illustrations below.

5.3.1 Maximum and cruising speeds

For any type of vehicle, the tractive power required *at the road*, for constant speed on level ground, is simply the sum of the aerodynamic and rolling resistance power terms. From equation (5.7)

$$P = \tfrac{1}{2} \rho\, V^3 A C_D + (W k_r) V. \tag{5.10}$$

The required total engine power output at any speed can be estimated by using the above expression, and factoring it up to take account of transmission losses. The transmission efficiency will be conservatively assumed to be 90%.

In figure 5.10, the power requirement has been calculated for the case study vehicle at two speeds, 113 km/h and 130 km/h, corresponding to the legal motorway speed limits in the UK and most Continental countries respectively. The power required, even for the worst case of 130 km/h fully loaded, is only

Speed (km/h)	113	130
Engine output power required driver only (kW)	17.7	25
Engine output power required fully loaded (kW)	22.2	27.3

Figure 5.10:   Engine power required for the example vehicle at constant speed on a level road.

27.3 kW. This would need to be increased a little to take account of heating, ventilation, cooling, and other electrical services. However, the resulting required engine power of around 30 kW is considerably less than the maximum engine output for a conventional vehicle of this class, which would typically be around 75 to 85 kW. The large discrepancy between the available power in a conventional car and the power required for cruising is partly due to marketing constraints. Owners like the idea of a car that can achieve at least 160 km/h, even though that speed may be illegal. Most of the excess power is, however, required for either acceleration or hill climbing. In a hybrid vehicle, these two latter functions can be aided by the use of stored energy, so a large engine becomes unnecessary. For equal power outputs, a small engine working at high load will normally be more efficient than a large engine on part load, as described elsewhere in this book.

5.3.2 Acceleration

The energy required to accelerate a vehicle can be obtained by integrating the power output over time. The variation in available power during acceleration may be quite complex, as the engine output changes with the engine speed, which in turn depends on the vehicle speed and the gearing. In vehicles with stepped changes in gear ratio, there will be corresponding step changes in power. At low speed, the amount of power that can be utilised is limited by the tendency of the wheels to spin. In addition, allowance must be made for the power that is absorbed in accelerating the rotating components. These can also be subject to step changes in rotational speed. The actual process of integration is quite straightforward using numerical means.

Figure 5.11 shows an energy breakdown obtained using a performance simulation programme developed by the authors. The vehicle data for our case study example have been used.   The computed data are for the case of a conventional vehicle with a manual transmission, accelerating as fast as possible

Hybrid Vehicle Propulsion

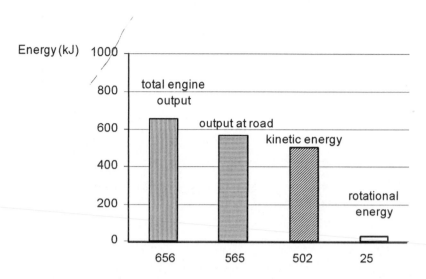

Figure 5.11:   Energy breakdown for a medium size car accelerating to 100 km/h in 12.2 s.

from rest to 100 km/h with driver only. The energy required to overcome the rotational inertia of the internal components and wheels has been taken as being equal to 5% of the linear kinetic energy of the vehicle ($\frac{1}{2} mV^2$). Any power required for auxiliaries has been ignored. The maximum engine output power was specified as 70 kW.

With this data, the total acceleration time was computed as 12.2 seconds, which is a typical value for 1.6 litre vehicles in this class.   From figure 5.11 it can be seen that of the 656 kJ produced by the motor, approximately 66 kJ is lost in the transmission, and a further 25 kJ is used to accelerate the rotating components, principally the wheels. Further losses occur due to rolling resistance and aerodynamic drag, so that the final kinetic energy of the vehicle is only 502 kJ. No allowance has been made for any energy absorbed by auxiliaries.

5.3.3 The use of stored energy to assist acceleration

In a hybrid vehicle, some of the overall energy can be drawn from storage, via a supplementary electric motor or other power transmission device. Therefore, the power output of the primary motor can be reduced. For the same maximum acceleration case as used previously, figure 5.12 shows how the required primary engine power changes with the amount of stored energy available. It has been assumed that the stored energy is released at such a rate as to replicate the acceleration characteristics of a conventionally powered vehicle. Clearly, as the size and power of the engine is increased, the amount of stored energy required

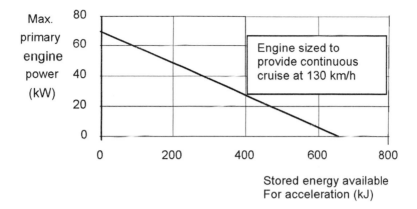

Figure 5.12:   The relationship between the amount of stored energy required and the primary engine power available for acceleration to 100 km/h in 12.2 s, for a 1300 kg vehicle.

for assistance is reduced, and the hybrid arrangement becomes 'milder', losing part of the benefit.

The figure also indicates the amount of stored energy that would be required for this acceleration if the selected primary engine were just powerful enough to maintain a steady speed of 130 km/h. As mentioned earlier, this would require around 27 kW.

The amount of stored energy needed to boost the acceleration in this case is quite small at 400 kJ. This is roughly the amount of energy that can be stored in a conventional car battery, although such a battery would in fact be completely unsuitable, for reasons that were discussed in Chapter 3. As shown later, however, acceleration may not be the critical factor in determining the amount of stored energy required.

5.3.4 Energy storage requirements for regenerative braking

In a conventional vehicle, the kinetic energy that a vehicle possesses is lost during braking. In a hybrid, however, at least part of this can be recovered by regenerative braking, where, instead of conventional friction brakes, resistance is provided by a generator that returns some of the energy to the storage device. Due to system inefficiencies, the proportion of braking energy recovered may be small. However, for a conventional car in urban driving conditions, up to 40% of the total energy supplied may be lost in braking, so there is considerable scope for energy savings by means of regenerative braking.

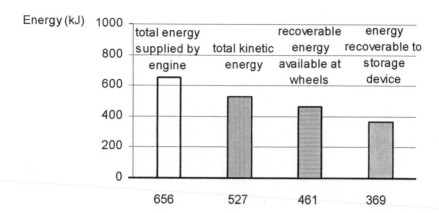

Figure 5.13: Energy breakdown (kJ) for the case-study vehicle decelerating from
            100 km/h.

The case study vehicle can be used to illustrate the order of magnitude of the
losses involved. The energy breakdown for this deceleration case is illustrated in
figure 5.13.

If we consider the case of the vehicle (with driver only) decelerating from
100 km/h, then prior to braking, the kinetic energy due to linear motion will be
502 kJ (as in figure 5.12). In addition the vehicle will possess rotational kinetic
energy due to the inertia of the rotating components, estimated as 25 kJ, (also as
in figure 5.12), so the total kinetic energy will be 527 kJ. If the deceleration and
acceleration rates are similar, the aerodynamic drag and wheel rolling resistance
will absorb roughly the same amount of energy during braking as was lost during
acceleration to 100 km/h (66 kJ), leaving 461 kJ available to be fed back into the
vehicle. The amount that can actually be converted and fed back into the storage
device will depend on both the transmission efficiency and the conversion
efficiency of the system. If this combined efficiency is 80%, then some 369 kJ
could be recovered to the storage device. This represents just 56% of the energy
originally supplied by the motor during acceleration. In practice, the ability to
absorb this amount of energy may be limited by the power acceptance capability
of the energy storage system. This, together with storage efficiency, is a major
consideration in the selection of the type of energy storage device. Batteries are
rather poor in this respect compared to flywheels.

A significant reduction in the required capacity of the energy storage device
can be obtained if it is decided that full regenerative braking from the maximum
speed $V_{(max)}$ is not required. This relaxation of the requirement is reasonable,
because under most normal driving conditions, a sudden stop from maximum

speed is seldom needed. Regenerative braking is most effective in stop-go or highly variable speed driving conditions.

A point that is not always readily appreciated is that if the energy storage device is to be used for regenerative braking, it must be sufficiently empty at the beginning of the braking phase. This means that if a vehicle starts off from rest with a fully charged unit, it will be necessary to use part of the stored energy immediately, otherwise there will be no capacity for regenerative storage. At any point in a journey, the storage devices must simultaneously have a sufficient 'source' of stored energy to supply the acceleration or hill climbing requirements, and a sufficient unused capacity 'sink' to receive the braking energy. These sink and source allocations are thus additive. The quantities of source and sink capacity vary throughout the journey, and optimising the total storage capacity is a complex task involving compromises. It also requires an analysis of the performance over complete driving cycles of the type illustrated in figure 5.7. The subject of control strategy in hybrid propulsion is dealt with in more detail in Chapter 6.

5.3.5 Hill climbing: a critical factor

At various stages in the journey, the energy requirement for hill climbing can be the most important factor in determining the energy storage requirement of a hybrid vehicle, particularly for long range out-of-town road vehicles. Figure 5.14 shows the normal maximum gradients used for different types of road.

ROAD TYPE	GRADIENT
Normal motorway	4%
Steep motorway usually with crawler lane	5%
Non-motorway dual carriageway	6%

Figure 5.14: Normal maximum road gradients.

The total engine output power required for the case study vehicle to ascend these gradients fully loaded (1800 kg) is shown in figure 5.15. It will be seen that an engine power of around 50 kW would be sufficient to allow the vehicle to ascend the 4% motorway gradient at a respectable 120 km/h, and a steep motorway at 100 km/h, a performance that would be just about acceptable. This order of engine power would have been typical for such a car a few years ago, but the demand for better acceleration has led to the provision of increasingly powerful motors. In a hybrid vehicle, it would be possible to fit a less powerful prime mover, and rely on some stored energy to assist in hill climbing. The

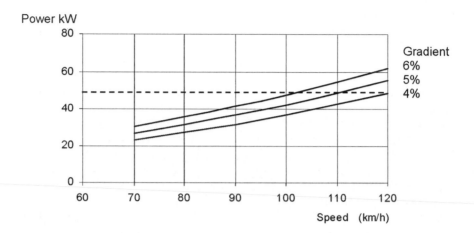

Figure 5.15:   The power required for the fully loaded example vehicle to ascend typical road gradients at various speeds.

amount of stored energy required depends on the length and gradient of the hill, the speed required, and the amount of primary engine power available.

Figure 5.16 shows the balance between amount of stored energy required, and the primary engine power available for the fully loaded case study vehicle attempting to ascend a 5% gradient 1 km long at 110 km/h.

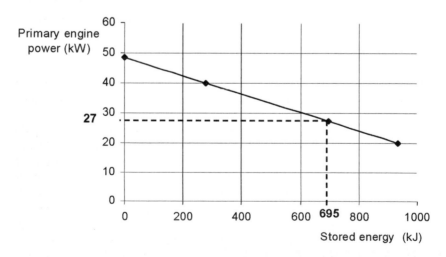

Figure 5.16:   The balance between stored energy required and main motor power available, for the fully laden example vehicle climbing a 1 km long 5% gradient hill at 110 km/h.

As indicated in figure 5.16, if the primary engine power were only 27.3 kW (the power required for motorway cruising at 130 km/h), the stored energy required would be 695 kJ. This is considerably larger than the amount that was required to provide sufficient boost for adequate acceleration to 100 km/h.

It may thus be seen that hill-climbing performance tends to be one of the most important factors in sizing the engine and energy storage capacity of mild hybrid road vehicles. It is a feature of most current designs that they are not ideally suited to use in mountainous terrain.

5.3.6 Hill descent

When a vehicle descends a hill, part of its initial potential energy may be recovered as stored energy if the means of preventing over-speeding on descent is by regenerative braking. The fully loaded case study vehicle descending the 1 km 5% gradient hill would lose a total of 883 kJ of potential energy. Of this, 546 kJ would be absorbed by aerodynamic drag and rolling resistance, leaving 337 kJ to be absorbed by regenerative braking. This mechanism provides yet another means by which a hybrid vehicle can improve upon the overall efficiency in comparison with a conventional car. Unfortunately, most of the standard driving cycles used as benchmarks for vehicle performance do not include any hill-climbing requirements, so neither the relative strengths nor the weaknesses of the hybrid will be fully revealed in the standard tests and simulations.

5.3.7 The final balance between continuous engine power and the power from stored energy

In a long-range hybrid vehicle, it is normal to size the prime mover to provide sufficient continuous power at least to sustain the design cruising speed on level ground without any use of stored energy. The stored energy is only used to provide acceleration and for hill-climbing. As discussed above, the hill-climbing ability can really dominate the requirement unless the vehicle is to be used in a substantially flat geographical location. In urban transport systems, prolonged ascent of gradients is seldom required.

In our example vehicle, a bare minimum of 27 kW primary engine power with a stored energy capacity of around 700 to 800 kJ would be necessary to maintain adequate hill climbing performance. In order to allow for the extra load required for heating, air conditioning and other services, and to provide a certain amount of reserve, a practical hybrid would undoubtedly need a more powerful engine. The primary engine of the Toyota Prius provides a fairly generous maximum power of 53 kW, which permits a maximum sustained speed of 160 km/h. This may seem excessive, but from a marketing point of view, it is necessary to convince customers that this new type of vehicle is not inferior to its conventional competitors. The customers' performance requirements will partly be a matter of geography. An owner living in the flat plains of North-Western Europe will generally have quite different needs from those of an Alpine resident, who might be better off with a conventional vehicle.

The Prius and the Insight have battery storage capacities of 6.4 and 3.36 MJ respectively, which is considerably greater than the minimum of 700 to 800 kJ estimated above. However, it should be remembered that with battery storage, it is necessary to have a large reserve of capacity in order to ensure an adequate charge/discharge cycle life. The figures above suggest that the Prius battery is only working within about 1/10 of its total capacity, which is in fact consistent with the requirement for adequate battery cycle life.

Flywheel energy storage systems do not require such a large reserve of capacity, but the specific energy is much lower than for a battery. As described in Chapter 7, flywheel systems have been found to be well suited to public transport vehicles, but if a flywheel system is contemplated for a mild hybrid car, then the lower energy density has to be taken into account. It may be preferable, in this case, to limit the use of energy storage primarily to assisting acceleration and providing regenerative braking. From figure 5.12 it may be seen that with 53 kW available from the prime mover, the usable energy storage required for acceleration would be only 200 kJ. This would necessitate a maximum storage capacity of at least 300 kJ. Energy densities of around 20 kJ/kg are realisable with advanced designs, so the flywheel unit would weigh about 15 kg. As described in Chapter 7, the problem of gyroscopic effects can be solved in the case of buses by mounting the unit in a cardanic suspension, but this adds to the space requirement. For private motorcars, an ultracapacitor is a more promising alternative to the battery. A further discussion of the storage options for a mild hybrid car is given in reference [5.4].

5.3.8 Performance over the complete cycle

Although a study of the elements of the performance cycle as given above gives some understanding of the energy storage and power requirements, the final design process requires a simulation of complete driving cycles. This is the only reliable method of predicting the performance characteristics, and for assessing the fuel consumption. Current production mild hybrids have the ability to temporarily switch off the prime mover during short stops, and it is in the simulation of the urban cycle that the benefits of this feature really show up in the fuel savings that result. Performance simulations are described in the next chapter.

5.4 Rail vehicle performance

For rail vehicles, the performance requirements may be specified with some precision, since speed and gradient information for a given network is usually available. The rolling resistance of rail vehicles is considerably lower than for road vehicles, which increases the proportion of energy that could be recovered by regenerative braking.

5.5 The high storage capacity hybrid

At the opposite end of the spectrum from the 'mybrid' lie vehicles that utilise a larger amount of stored energy, and a smaller prime mover. Currently this arrangement is mostly used for urban public transport or utility services such as buses and small fleet delivery vehicles, and almost exclusively in urban areas. The sizing of the energy storage capacity and the recharging motor is based on an 'energy management' approach. It is necessary to ensure that at any point on a journey cycle, the amount of energy in the storage device lies between its maximum and permitted lower limits. The stored energy at any instant depends on the total history of the journey, as represented in figure 5.17.

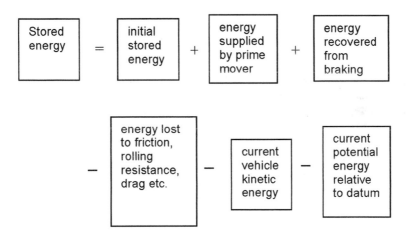

Figure 5.17: The stored energy in a hybrid vehicle.

Figure 5.18 shows a simulated example of a stored energy availability chart for a short section of urban driving with cycles involving acceleration, steady speed and regenerative braking. The vehicle starts with the storage unit charged with 500 kJ of energy, and this is topped up by a small motor working at a steady 16 kW. The first four stages are labelled. The stored energy drops rapidly as the vehicle initially accelerates. It then rises slowly during the cruise phase. During braking, energy is recovered. While the vehicle is stopped, the prime mover continues to top up the stored energy.

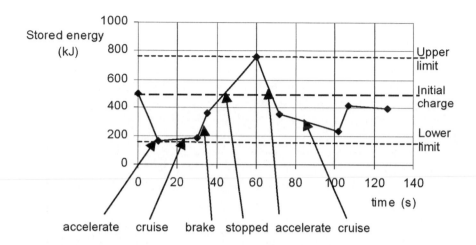

Figure 5.18:   Stored energy availability for a hybrid vehicle with a constant steady energy input from the motor, and regenerative braking.

In this illustrative example the energy level has stayed within the specified limits. If the upper limit is reached, charging must cease, and the motor must either idle or stop. If the lower limit is approached, the vehicle must slow down. It will be seen that for a high level of optimisation, the details of likely journeys must be predicted accurately. In practice, it is normal to make the charging motor sufficiently large to drive the vehicle at a reasonable minimum get-you-home speed.   Most practical hybrid vehicles of this type have a motor that is sufficiently powerful to supply the daily energy requirements, thus obviating the need for external recharging.

Figure 5.18 simply illustrates the basic principle of energy management. The design and optimisation of a real vehicle will of course involve a much more complex driving cycle than that shown, and many more factors have to be taken into consideration in designing the system. The processes of design optimisation are discussed further in the following chapter.

5.6 References

[5.1]   Barnard, R. H., *Road Vehicle Aerodynamic Design*, Longman, ISBN 0-582-24522-2, 1996.
[5.2]   Hucho, W-H., *Aerodynamics of Road Vehicles*, Butterworth, London, 1987.

[5.3]   Buckley, F. T., Marks, C. H. and Watson, W. N., A study of aerodynamic methods for improving fuel economy, *US National Science Foundation, final report, SIA 74 14843*, University of Maryland, Dept. of Mechanical Engineering, 1978.

[5.4]   Barnard, R. H. and Jefferson, C. M., Criteria for sizing the prime mover and energy storage capacity in hybrid vehicles. *Proc. 30th. ISATA Conference On Electric And Hybrid Vehicles*, Florence, June 16-19, 1997.

Chapter 6

CONTROL STRATEGIES

6.1 Modelling and simulation of hybrid vehicle performance

In order to design and evaluate hybrid propulsion systems and test control strategies, it helps initially to analyse the performance over one element of a drive cycle, namely: acceleration - cruise - deceleration - standstill. To an approximation, most urban drive cycles can be considered as a sequence of such elemental cycles.

The theoretical power demand on the propulsion system was discussed in Chapter 5. Figure 6.1 shows the results from a performance simulation programme developed by the authors. The results show the predicted performance of the hybrid bus developed by CCM, (described in Chapter 7), accelerating at 1 m/s^2 to a speed of 50 km/h, subject to a power limit of 150 kW, and covering a distance of 500 m between stops. This is a fairly typical duty cycle for an urban bus operation. This bus has a 35 kW, 2 litre car engine as prime mover and flywheel energy storage of 93% efficiency. The traction efficiency was assumed to be 90%, which is readily achievable with modern power electronic drives. The simulation model is described in detail by Jefferson and Ackerman [6.1].

The effect of the specified power limit is a slight but tolerable reduction in the average acceleration. The results also indicate that for this cycle, 35 kW of prime mover power is adequate, since the stored energy is replenished by the time the vehicle is stationary. The engine is thus sized for the average power demand [6.2].

6.2 Full performance analysis and assessment

It cannot be assumed that the vehicle duty cycle will consist simply of a succession of cycles of the type shown in figure 6.1. The prime mover power will normally have to be varied over the course of the journey. To fully assess the suitability of the control system, it will be necessary to analyse the vehicle performance over a realistic journey. The standard US and European driving cycles may not be adequate for this purpose, as they are really intended as a basis for comparing fuel consumption, and do not necessarily represent a typical journey in any detail.

Hybrid Vehicle Propulsion

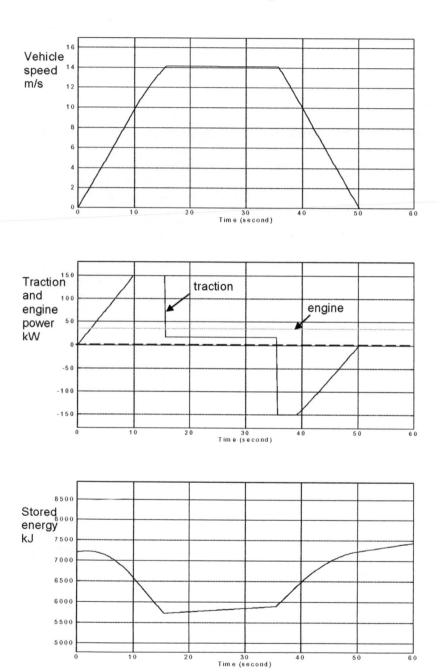

Figure 6.1: Simulated hybrid bus start-stop cycle over a 500 m distance.

6.3 Control systems

The hybrid configuration, as shown in figure 6.2, allows for a range of possible strategies for control of the power flow. In a series hybrid electric vehicle, the DC link provides the interconnection for power flow between the components. The question is, how is the voltage set? This depends on the individual electronic control units, which are shown in figure 6.1 as a converter, on each element. In practice, to avoid conflict, one component needs to dominate the others. In battery hybrids, the batteries are often connected directly to the DC link, in which case they determine the voltage, otherwise they would be stressed. The rest of the electrical system must work to that voltage.

In flywheel systems, the flywheel unit and its converter emulate the battery. This requires a fairly intelligent form of control, by which the function of the unit is to hold the DC link voltage steady, otherwise variation in the DC link voltage could affect the power flow in the traction motors and prime mover.

In the case of the gas turbine generator, the power is very sensitive to changes in the DC link voltage. Controlling this is therefore very important. In the gas turbine/flywheel project (ULEV-TAP) [6.3] the DC link voltage was indeed held steady at a controlled set point by the flywheel control system, but the set point

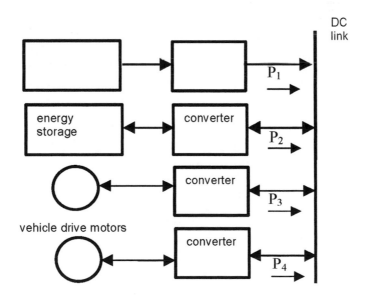

Figure 6.2: Series hybrid electric configuration.

was varied in order to control the gas turbine electrical power output. This in turn varied the mechanical load on the gas turbine. The gas turbine speed was regulated by a governor so that the fuel rate was adjusted automatically. The traction power was controlled independently, but it was up to the flywheel controller to ensure that surges in traction power did not affect the DC link voltage. This meant that the flywheel power controller had to respond immediately to changes in the traction power, since any upset in the power balance would sharply affect the DC link voltage. The DC link therefore not only formed a channel for power flow but also an effective means on control and communication between the system components. Control of the DC link voltage is thus an essential feature of the control strategy of most series hybrid electric vehicles. In this configuration, the DC link provides the power interface between the components. Kirchhoff's law, known to electrical engineers, states what is almost obvious here, that the sum of the currents, and therefore the levels of power flow into the DC link, must be zero. Therefore:

$$P_1 + P_2 + P_3 + P_4 = 0.$$

This is by way of saying that the DC link itself cannot continuously accumulate or dissipate power.

This equation may be arithmetically simple, but it conceals the fact that one power level must be determined by the other three. Which one is the dependent, is a function of the control strategy. Presumably, we would wish the driver to determine the power in the traction motors at any point in time. This power must be delivered by the prime mover and energy storage unit together. The power balance between the two provides a degree of freedom which can be adapted to follow various strategies. These are usually aimed at optimising the operating conditions of the engine or prime mover, taking into account the operational constraints of the energy storage unit.

The DC link is not the only way of transmitting power in a series electrical hybrid vehicle. An alternative strategy has been developed by CCM in the Netherlands [6.4]. Here, the traction motors, energy storage and prime mover are arranged in series so that they form a current loop, as in figure 6.3. In this arrangement there is no fixed voltage but each component draws the same current by use of current source inverters. These have an advantage over the voltage source inverters, which are needed to control power into the DC link, in that they have a much lower switching frequency. Thus, more cost effective and efficient electronic switching can be used. The flywheel bus developed by CCM employs this current loop control system. As a result, the flywheel unit has a storage efficiency of 93%, which is probably higher than any other storage systems currently available. The control strategy can be more or less the same as with the DC link. The controller shown in figure 6.3 is used to control the power in the energy storage unit. The power in the traction motors is controlled by the vehicle driver.

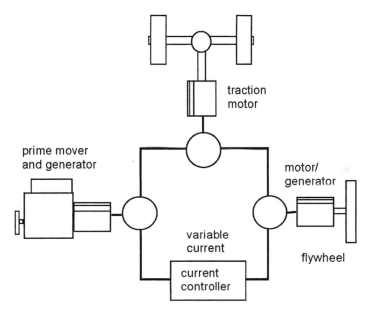

Figure 6.3: Current loop serial arrangement of electrical transmission.

The power in the prime mover makes up the difference, but as with the DC link, the power in the energy storage unit can be intelligently controlled so as to keep the prime mover power at its optimal level. The series hybrid electric configuration has been taken as a case for explanation, but the same basic control principles apply equally to all hybrid configurations.

6.4 Control strategies

There are several basic optional control strategies, and the choice is determined largely by the choice of target operational parameters for the particular vehicle duty cycle. These will usually include the fuel efficiency, but quietness of operation, or the need to avoid excessive cycling of components such as the battery may often be major considerations. The basic main options for control strategy are as below.

6.4.1 Run the prime mover continuously at full power

This would lead to considerable fuel wastage, particularly when the vehicle is stationary, running at slow speed or running downhill, since excess energy would need to be dissipated.

6.4.2 Run the prime mover continuously at optimum power

This is usually less than full power, and would require a higher rated unit to achieve the same performance. There is a strategic element to selecting the optimum power of a prime mover, depending on whether the aim is to minimise fuel consumption, engine wear or emissions. If the aim is to reduce emissions, then a decision has to be made as to which combustion product is to be minimised. This will depend very much on the prime mover characteristics and, to some extent, on the operational specifications that need to be met. Though fuel consumption and emissions may be reduced, there may still be some fuel wastage, as in case 1.

6.4.3 Logic control 'on-off'

The prime mover would be run at its optimum power, until the stored energy is up to capacity, at which time the prime mover is turned off. It is turned on again when the available stored energy is depleted to a specified threshold level. This addresses the problem of energy wastage, but lacks the intelligence as to the anticipated energy requirements of the vehicle. For example, the stored energy could be nearly depleted at the time when acceleration is required. One could refine this by tightening the zone between the threshold stored energy levels at which prime mover switching occurs, according to the characteristic law shown in figure 6.4.

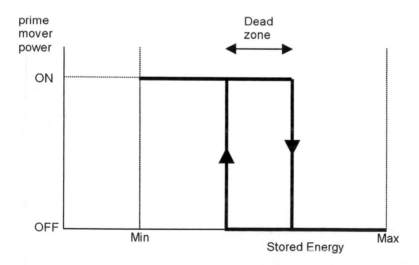

Figure 6.4: Logic control of prime mover power based on stored energy.

The dead zone is the band of stored energy level in which the prime mover remains in its existing 'on' or 'off' state. In the case of an internal combustion engine, the 'on' state would correspond to optimum power and the 'off' state would be with the engine idling, or, if permitted, turned off.

The problem with this approach is that the tighter the dead zone band, the higher the frequency of the prime mover 'on-off' cycles. This can result in thermal cycling which may reduce the engine efficiency and lifetime. If the prime mover is a diesel engine, gas turbine or fuel cell, such operation would probably not be practical.

6.4.4 Continuous control

Even though a prime mover will have an optimum operating point at a certain speed and torque, it may be preferable to adopt a strategy which allows deviation from this point for the sake of reducing wear. A spark ignition engine has an efficiency map typically of the form shown in figure 6.5. Diesel engines show a similar characteristic map, but the efficiency is less sensitive to speed variation.

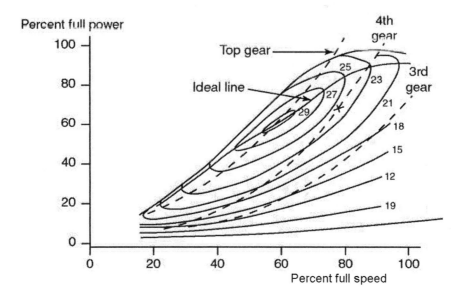

Figure 6.5: A typical efficiency map for a spark ignition engine, with efficiency contours shown in percentages.

The optimum operating point on this example is at about 60% full power at 60% full speed. In a series hybrid, the power output and engine speed can be adjusted by a combination of the throttle setting and the load applied by the control system. In a parallel hybrid, the speed can be controlled directly by the gearbox or CVT. By thus controlling the speed and power, it is possible to keep the operating point close to the ideal line locus shown in figure 6.5. As long as this condition is met, then it may be seen that deviations of speed and power of about 20% from the optimum point do not produce an appreciable loss in efficiency.

It may be noted that in a conventional vehicle, the power required is determined by the driving condition, and as may be seen from figure 6.5, if the power demand is low, the efficiency will be poor. In a hybrid, the load may be increased, at least temporarily, by recharging the storage device. This lack of direct connection between the prime mover power and the power required by the driving condition, allows the prime mover of the hybrid vehicle to be operated at close to the ideal line for a far greater proportion of the time than is the case with conventional transmission.

A simple strategy for continuous control, would be to vary the prime mover by the control law

$$\text{Power} = \text{gain} \ (E_1 - E_2)$$

where E_1 is the mid band level of stored energy
and E_2 is the actual level.

This is a form of error proportional feedback control. The power is set at a level proportional to the error in the stored energy: i.e. the difference between this and the mid band value. The aim of this strategy is to maintain the stored energy at or near its mid band level, so as to maintain the capacity of the storage unit to discharge or absorb power. The gain is a parameter setting. The higher the gain, the closer the control, but the less stable will be the prime mover power.

The response of the system to a typical start stop cycle might be as shown in figure 6.6. This figure shows the time histories of the vehicle speed, the traction power, the stored energy and the prime mover power. With this form of control, there is a trade-off between the high gain setting, which would result in close control of the stored energy, but with a high amplitude and frequency of variation in the prime mover power; or a low gain, which may not keep the stored energy within its desired limits.

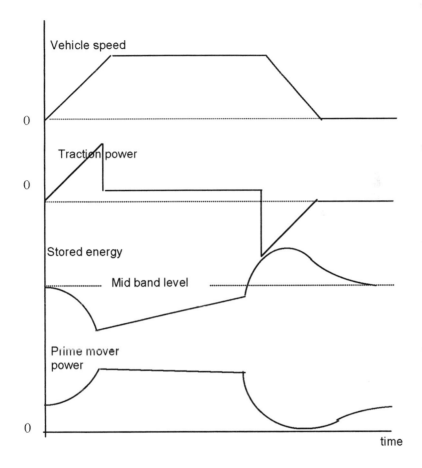

Figure 6.6: Response of error proportional control of stored energy.

A more intelligent form of control has been developed for a gas turbine - flywheel hybrid system for a light rail vehicle [6.3]. Here a proportional + integral (P+I) controller is used, as shown in figure 6.7. This effectively sets the prime mover power to the value of the traction power filtered over a 1000 second period. This avoids the prime mover having to respond rapidly to changes in the traction power, but responds slowly to changing trends in traction power due, say, to a change in average speed or gradient.

In order to control the energy storage facility over the long term, the sum of the vehicle kinetic energy and stored energy is monitored, and kept constant by feeding an error signal based on this total energy, relative to a set point, forward to the prime mover control. This provides some bias in the controller output, which trims the prime mover power so as to reduce this error, by adjusting the

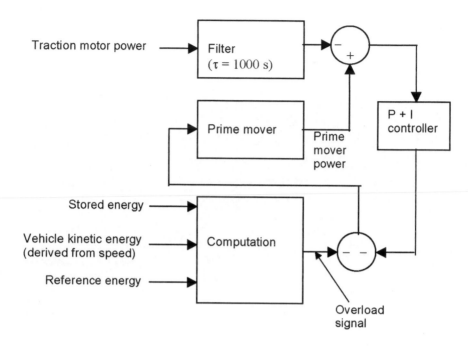

Figure 6.7:   P + I control of prime mover power.

mean stored energy accordingly. In this way, the prime mover power is adjusted gradually, so as to both compensate for changes in the external load on the traction motors, and also to keep the flywheel speed within specified limits.

The control system is designed to manage the stored energy in such a way that its limits are not exceeded, and also so that the prime mover power only has to vary gradually, to avoid rapid cycling. Because the total energy only varies gradually, this form of control is a feasible option.

6.5 The management of battery hybrid systems

For battery hybrid vehicles, such as the Toyota Prius, it is the battery power which needs careful management so as to avoid excessive cycling and deep discharge. This vehicle, however, has a petrol engine, which is well suited to cycling. The control strategy is thus rather different, and can be biased towards protecting the battery. The strategy involved will depend on the battery type but, in general, frequent cycling and deep discharge reduce its storage efficiency and lifetime and should thus be avoided. This tends to mean that accelerating the vehicle should not discharge the battery by more than 80%. Even with that limited depth of discharge, the battery life is limited to 3 years in normal driving conditions.

Some new types of lead-acid battery exhibit ultracapacitor type characteristics, which can be exploited to good effect by appropriate battery management strategy. However, discussion in detail on such strategies is beyond the scope of this text.

Gas turbine battery hybrids have been investigated, but the problem here is that neither component should be subject to cycling, and this presents a dilemma in control system design. For this reason, a gas turbine flywheel option seems a better alternative, and this arrangement was adopted in the ULEV-TAP light rail vehicle described in the next chapter.

Fuel cell battery hybrids may well present the same problem, because fuel cells are susceptible to thermal cycling, and reformers are incapable of responding rapidly to changes in power demand. The remedy may be to resort to flywheel energy storage or to supplement the batteries with ultracapacitor storage, which can be cycled hard, and has a high specific power. In this case, it would be necessary to have a strategy for controlling the ultracapacitor power, in addition to the battery and fuel cell power. As with the example of flywheel energy storage, the ultracapacitor power would need to follow the rapid variations in traction power, in order to take the cycling out of the fuel cell and battery.

6.6 Control strategy and route dependence

In the strategies discussed so far, we have assumed that the energy storage capacity is always sufficient. This may not be the case when exceptional vehicle speeds or extended distances on gradients are required. A strategy is needed to cope with these eventualities. On rail vehicles, speeds and gradients are fairly predictable. By intelligent control of the prime mover power set point, the energy storage can be charged in anticipation of an upward gradient or requirement for higher speed. It can similarly be allowed to discharge in advance of a downward gradient. This is generally not the case with road vehicles, but with experience the driver can adapt his driving technique to anticipate the demands of hill climbing or rapid acceleration.

6.7 References

[6.1]   Jefferson, C. M. and Ackerman, M., A flywheel variator energy storage system, *Energy Conversion and Management*, Vol. 37, No. 10, pp. 1481-1491, 1996.

[6.2]   Barnard, R. H. and Jefferson, C. M., Criteria for sizing the prime mover and energy storage capacity in hybrid vehicles, 30th ISATA Conference, *Proceedings of Electric, Hybrid and Alternative Fuel Vehicles*, Florence, June 1997, No. 97EL027, pp. 363-370.

[6.3]   Lohner, A., Berndt, J., Schülting, L. and Zeher, S., Intelligent power management of an ultra-low emission light-rail vehicle using a gas turbine supply and flywheel powered electric propulsion, *Proceedings of the PROSPER Congress*, Karlsruhe, 19-20 September 2001, www.prosper.ttk.de

[6.4]   Smits, E., Huisman, H. and Thoolen, F., A hybrid city bus using an electro mechanical accumulator for power demand smoothing. *Proceedings of the European Power Electronics Conference*, Vol. 4, Trondheim, 1997.

Chapter 7

CASE ILLUSTRATIONS

7.1 Categories of hybrid vehicles covered

Thus far, hybrid vehicle have mainly fallen into three categories, namely:

1. domestic cars
2. buses
3. rail vehicles

   In this chapter we will give examples of hybrid vehicles from each of the above categories that have been marketed, operated or extensively tested. Reference will also be made to some promising proposals. A fourth category comprising commercial vehicles including off-roaders could be considered, but so far, there has only been a limited amount of development work on hybrid versions of such vehicles.

7.2 Hybrid domestic cars

The earliest full-scale production cars were the Toyota Prius and the Honda Insight. These were both of the mild hybrid type, that is, with limited energy storage. This does seem to be the trend for domestic cars, and no significant production series-hybrid battery-electric domestic car has yet emerged. Both of these production vehicles used nickel-metal hydride batteries for the energy storage, although the experimental forerunner of the Insight, the JVX, used an ultracapacitor, as mentioned below. As yet, no major manufacturer has shown any enthusiasm for the flywheel for this vehicle class, which is a pity because the flywheel required for a mild hybrid would be a very small and compact unit. Future mild hybrids may well use advanced lead-acid batteries instead of Ni-MH, as the weight penalty is not particularly high.

   Following encouraging feedback from sales of the Prius and Insight cars, both manufacturers have embarked on further projects using the same basic technologies. We will start by describing these two vehicles.

7.2.1 The Toyota Prius

The Prius, shown in figure 7.1, was the first large-scale production battery mild hybrid domestic car. It uses a 1.5 litre 53 kW petrol engine and a 33 kW electric motor with a 6.4 MJ (1.78 kWh) 274 V nickel-metal hydride battery for energy storage. The petrol engine is designed for high efficiency rather than high specific power.

Figure 7.1:   The Toyota Prius petrol/electric hybrid. A fuel consumption of 62 mpg on the urban cycle makes this vehicle an attractive option for city use.   (Photo R. H. Barnard.)

The Prius has a relatively sophisticated hybrid arrangement, which the manufacturers designate as THS (Toyota Hybrid System). Details of the configuration are given in Chapter 2. This is really a mixture of parallel and series arrangements. Power can be delivered mechanically from the i.c. engine, with assistance being provided by the battery and electric drive motor, as in a parallel arrangement. Alternatively, it can function in series mode, with the i.c. engine driving a generator connected electrically to the electric drive motor and battery. In general, it tends to act in a blend of the two modes.

The drive train is described and illustrated in Chapter 2, and shown in figure 7.2. Power from the petrol engine is fed to the wheels via an ingenious form of differential, which uses an epicyclic gear train to mix the power flows from the petrol engine and the electric motor/generator, and allows it to provide a continuously variable speed transmission (CVT). There is thus no gear change lever; the driver simply moves a selector lever as on a conventional automatic. The system is described in a little more detail by Bursa [7.1]. Not surprisingly, the propulsion and transmission package produces quite a complex and tight-fitting arrangement in the engine bay, as may be seen in figure 7.3.

Figure 7.2: The engine, control unit and differential gear unit of the Toyota Prius.

Figure 7.3: The engine bay of the Prius.

The Prius is a comfortable medium to small family car (by European standards) with a high level of equipment including air conditioning. The first obvious feature when driving the vehicle is the absence of any cranking noise when the engine starts. When the ignition key is turned, the electrical drive system simply brings the petrol engine smoothly up to running speed. The low-revving engine is almost inaudible. Depending on the initial state of charge of the battery, the car will normally start off under electric power, thereby releasing storage capacity for later regenerative braking. If the accelerator pedal is fully depressed, power will be taken from the petrol engine as well, and at this point, the engine becomes audible. Acceleration is similar to that in comparable conventional cars. During short stops with the selector lever in the drive position, the engine will normally shut off, and then restart when required.

An interesting feature of the interior of the vehicle is an illuminated display on the dashboard. This schematically shows changes in the direction of the power flows as seen in figure 7.4. The fuel consumption rate can also be displayed. On a journey of around three miles in a suburban area in light traffic after a cold start, undertaken by one of the authors, a figure of 55 mpg was returned. Toyota literature gives the urban cycle fuel consumption as 4.6 litres/100 km (61.4 UK mpg), and the combined cycle consumption as 5.9 litres/100 km (57.6 UK mpg). This is an interesting reversal of the trend in conventional cars where the combined cycle normally shows a better fuel consumption than the urban cycle.

Figure 7.4:   The illuminated dashboard display of the Prius, which shows the varying power flow directions.

The high fuel efficiency of the Prius in urban use is evident, and is produced by a combination of the effects of operating the engine at an efficient load and speed setting, regenerative braking, the very low engine power consumption during idling, and the fact that the petrol engine is normally switched off during short stops. CO_2 emissions are quoted as 114 g/km, which may be compared with the 180 g/km or more of a good equivalent conventional car. This level falls well within the 150 g/km limit of the lowest CO_2 emissions category specified in the UK VED taxation categories. Maximum acceleration to 100 km/h (62 mph) takes 13.4 seconds, which may not look impressive compared to a typical manual transmission vehicle, but it should be remembered that quoted acceleration figures for manual transmission cars are obtained by skilled test drivers 'thrashing' the gearbox. With an automatic, the maximum acceleration can be obtained by any driver, with no effort or skill. The maximum speed is around 160 km/h (100 mph).

The generator provides adequate resistance for light braking, and indeed, the brake pedal needs quite a light touch compared to some conventional vehicles. In the UK, the car attracts some Government subsidy, and it benefits from being eligible for a special low road tax. The Prius is competitively priced in the UK, but this is partly due to the subsidy, and partly due to generous discounting by the manufacturers who are keen to promote the technology.

7.2.2 The Honda Insight

The Honda Insight shown in figure 7.5 is a less complicated form of hybrid than the Toyota Prius.

Figure 7.5: The Honda Insight hybrid.

The Honda system is called IMA (integrated motor assist) by the manufacturers, and consists of a very thin compact reversible motor/generator interposed between a 1 litre, 3 cylinder, direct injection petrol engine and a 5 speed manual gearbox and final drive unit.

The electric motor can be used to provide a power boost during acceleration, and is used as a starter motor to run the i.c. engine up smoothly to operating speed. It can also act as a generator, and thus provide regenerative braking. A 144 V nickel-metal hydride battery of 3.36 MJ (0.94 kWh) capacity is used. A separate 12 V battery is used for lighting and accessories. The engine bay is just as crowded as that of the Prius, as may be seen in figure 7.6.

Figure 7.6: The engine bay of the Honda Insight.

The Insight is a small 2-seat sports vehicle with a light aluminium body weighing a mere 850 kg, and has an extremely low drag coefficient of 0.25. The EU combined cycle fuel consumption is claimed to be 3.4 litres/100 km (83 UK mpg) with an extra-urban cycle consumption of 3 litres/100 km (94.2 UK mpg). This impressively low fuel consumption will clearly be partly due to the low weight and drag, but the regenerative braking will also have a major impact. A final important contribution comes from the fact that the engine normally switches off when the vehicle is brought to rest in neutral. Depressing the clutch to engage first gear automatically restarts the motor. The CO_2 emissions are quoted as 80 g/km, which is around half the figure that might be expected for a new model of an equivalent conventional car.

A small three cylinder engine would normally produce a somewhat 'rough' power output at low speeds, but the IMA system compensates by using the electrical unit to smooth the output torque. Despite the small size of the prime mover, acceleration to 100 km/h (62 mph) requires only 12.5 seconds, and a top speed of 180 km/h (112 mph) is attainable.

A direct forerunner to the Insight was the J-VX prototype car, which was shown at the 1997 Tokyo Motor Show. The same engine and IMA system was employed, but an ultracapacitor was used instead of the Ni-MH battery. Ultracapacitor technology was presumably not considered to be sufficiently developed for use in a production vehicle. The choice of a manual gearbox may seem a little surprising for a hybrid vehicle, but it does have the advantage of high efficiency, and Honda were also no doubt mindful of the resistance to automatic cars in Europe, particularly for vehicles with sporting pretensions.

The Insight is clearly intended to act as a large-scale experiment to test both the technical practicality and the sales potential of this novel concept. Following encouraging results, Honda intends to introduce the IMA into its mainstream cars. Further details of both the Insight and the Prius are given by Dettmer [7.2].

7.2.3 The future outlook for the hybrid car

The Honda IMA arrangement is a less radical departure from the conventional than the Toyota system, and with the predicted move to 42/36 V electrical systems for conventional cars, it may represent the first step towards what will become the norm for the next generation of vehicles. The 42 V generators are likely to have a power rating of at least 5 kW, and at this level, it would be advantageous to make them integral with the drive shaft, as in the IMA system. The use of the same unit to act as the starter motor follows logically, as does the exploitation of the system to provide regenerative braking.

Toyota has also introduced a 'milder' form of hybrid drive, the THS-M. This involves a belt-driven motor/generator unit with a 36 V secondary battery and a high-efficiency petrol engine. It is similar in concept to the Honda IMA. Stop/start operation of the engine helps to reduce fuel consumption during urban use, and provides the same quiet start as the full THS system used in the Prius. Belt-driven motor/generator based hybrid systems appear to represent an intermediate step, and in the longer term, fully integrated arrangements such as the Honda IMA are likely to dominate. This motor-assist arrangement requires little extra cost when fitted to 42/36 V vehicles, and represents a straightforward evolutionary process. The more sophisticated arrangement of the THS system used on the Prius has the advantage of providing a stepless automatic transmission, and also the possibility of short-duration operation in urban areas designated as zero-emission zones.

7.3 Hybrid buses

Hybrid buses have attracted a considerable amount of interest, as they are seen as a useful weapon in the campaign to reduce urban pollution. Compared to alternative public transport options, the hybrid bus has the advantages of requiring no major infrastructure investment. It also produces a better overall well-to-wheel efficiency than electrical mains-powered vehicles such as trolleybuses. The hybrid bus also potentially offers a number of additional advantages compared to conventional buses. These may be listed as:

1. higher fuel efficiency
2. lower emissions
3. limited zero emission capability
4. lower noise levels
5. the possibility of using low floors throughout, thus aiding access
6. smooth stepless transmission.

A number of in-service evaluations have been undertaken around the world, particularly in Europe and Brazil. In many cases, operators have used lead-acid batteries for energy storage, as this was considered to represent a low risk approach.

The battery-based hybrid vehicles have shown a wide variation in their effectiveness in terms of fuel consumption. This seems to be due to variations in their level of technical development and optimisation. In some cases, the fuel efficiency of the hybrid test vehicles was slightly worse than that of a conventional bus, but in other cases reductions in fuel consumption of up to 15% have been demonstrated. Clearly, as the technology develops, hybrid battery-electric buses should show even greater gains.

In all cases, even those with relatively low fuel efficiency, emissions other than NO_x have been found to be significantly lower. Improved comfort and lower noise levels were achieved in all but one set of tests. There has also been some operational testing and evaluation of vehicles with flywheel energy storage, and these show even more encouraging results.

In the following section we will describe operational experience with a number of hybrid vehicles. It should be appreciated that during these trials, comparisons were made between experimental or partially developed vehicles and highly developed conventional buses. Unsurprisingly, the fuel efficiency of the hybrid vehicles was not in all cases much better, and reliability problems were sometimes encountered, particularly with battery storage. Fortunately there have now been sufficient trials where battery failures have not been a problem, to demonstrate that this is a development factor rather than an inherent weakness.

7.3.1 Operational trials of hybrid battery-electric buses in Terni, Italy
(after Alessandrini and Luca [7.3])

An analysis of trials of a number of hybrid battery electric buses is provided by Alessandrini and Luca [7.3]. The major part of this reference is devoted to a study of the operation of two models of hybrid bus in the Italian city of Terni. With the permission of the authors, some of the results of this study are given

Figure 7.7: An ALTRA hybrid diesel-battery bus.

below. The trials were conducted as a pilot project with the acronym FLEETS (Friendly Low Energy and Environmental Transport Systems), co-financed by the EC DG XVII under the THERMIE programme, and included amongst its partners, the local public transport company ATC and the Italian energy research and development institution ENEA.

The hybrid buses were put into service between the years 1997 and 1998 and were evaluated from both the technical and the social point of view. Four hybrid buses were manufactured by IVECO on designs produced by ALTRA. An example of an ALTRA hybrid bus is shown in figure 7.7. Salient features were:

Chassis	from the popular IVECO 490 bus.
Prime mover	Sofim 2800 Euro 2 supercharged diesel.
Transmission	purely electrical.
Electric traction motor	three-phase induction motor with a maximum output of 164 kW. It could also be used as a regenerative electric brake.
Alternator	water-cooled permanent magnet synchronous type coupled directly to the motor.
Battery charging regulator	IGBT air-cooled system that had to ensure that the generator worked at constant power under all operating conditions.
Drive control (inverter)	air-cooled GTO system with slippage control and continuous regulation of voltage and frequency.
Batteries	lead-acid, initially open type, but later replaced by sealed units with higher efficiency, better recovery, and lower maintenance requirements.

Technical results

The first important finding was that 37% of the electrical energy supplied to the traction motor was recovered by regenerative braking. It was also found that the traction motors used some 20% less energy than was supplied by the generator, the discrepancy being due to losses in the process of battery charge and discharge. Only 40% of the generated energy went directly to the traction motor, the other 60% went into charging the battery, and a significant proportion of this would thus have been lost due to the inefficiencies of the battery charge and discharge process. The overall system efficiency, starting from the fuel calorific value, was 27%, which is comparable with the 30% efficiency found on a conventional vehicle. This figure does not however include any account of the energy supplied during recharging at the depot from mains electricity.

	Mean values (l/km)	Standard deviation (l/km)
Conventional diesel bus	0.4370	0.856
Hybrid (measured consumption)	0.4407	0.1211
Hybrid (equivalent consumption)	0.4066	0.0932

Figure 7.8: Statistical results for comparative fuel consumption (after [7.3]).

It was concluded, that the average generator output power was greater than necessary, and that if this had been optimised, the fuel consumption could have been reduced by some 10%. Figure 7.8 gives a comparison between the hybrid bus and a conventional vehicle, and with a predicted equivalent consumption for the hybrid with an optimised charging rate.

	Diesel		Hybrid	
	Mean (g/km)	standard deviation (g/km)	Mean (g/km)	Standard deviation (g/km)
VOC	0.8212	0.6534	0.5875	0.8219
CO	5.0488	1.5021	0.2979	0.2517
NOx	24.9177	5.6787	11.5538	3.4768

Figure 7.9:   Comparison of emissions for the Terni hybrid and conventional diesel buses (after [7.3]).

As may be seen from figure 7.9, comparison of emissions was rather more encouraging than the fuel efficiency survey, but statistical uncertainties resulted from measurement problems that were associated with making measurements on a fully operational vehicle with passengers. This applies particularly to the VOC measurements. The CO and NOx trends are more reliable. The fact that large improvements are obtained despite no improvement in overall efficiency shows the benefits of running the engine at a more constant loading.

Reliability
The hybrid vehicles were less reliable than the conventional buses, as might have been expected from relatively undeveloped experimental vehicles. An analysis showed that nearly half (49%) of breakdowns were due to battery problems, with a further 37% being attributable to electrical and electronic devices. Only 13% were due to mechanical failures, and 1% to other causes. It was felt that the battery problems could be reduced by improvements to the electronic control systems, but it was clear that for widespread implementation it would be necessary to use batteries specifically designed for hybrid applications such as those used in the Prius and Insight cars.

Social evaluation
A group of 320 users was interviewed and asked to rank aspects of the hybrid bus operation on a scale of 1 (low) to 5 (high). The comfort of hybrid buses was ranked at 3.7, reduction in noise at 4.3, and reduction in pollution at 4.7. These results show that the travelling public was impressed by the hybrid buses.

7.3.2 Hybrid bus trials in Rome (after Alessandrini and Luca [7.3])

A set of 12 IVECO 490 hybridised buses identical to those tested in Terni was also evaluated on a single route in Rome. The buses were introduced in July 1999 up to November, operated at a regularity of around 95%. This compares unfavourably with conventional diesel buses which normally achieve a regularity of 99% when new, dropping to around 97% at ten years old. The problems, as in Terni, were mainly battery-related. By December, regularity had dropped to 92.7%, which led the operators to temporarily suspend trials. The cause of this decline was premature battery ageing. In the following January the buses were reintroduced with new maintenance-free battery packs using spiral cell technology, and regularity improved to an acceptable 98.5%. Unfortunately the battery problem had not been solved, and regularity fell off within four months, again due to premature battery ageing. Emission levels other than for NOx were found to be good, as indicated in figure 7.10.

	Level (g/kWh)	Euro III (g/kWh)
VOC	0.14	0.66
CO	0.14	2
NOx	8.03	7

Figure 7.10:   Emission figures for the Rome hybrid buses (after [7.3]).

7.3.3 Hybrid bus trials in Ferrara, Italy   (after Alessandrini and Luca [7.3])

The public transport company in Ferrara (Italy) bought eight hybrid buses similar to those in Terni and Rome, but with an impaired mobility access system installed on the rear door. The trial was motivated in part by a desire to reduce the noise vibration and the impact of noxious emissions on the fine Renaissance buildings in the city centre. Operational experiences were similar to those in Terni and Rome, with problems due to premature battery ageing. In addition, the air-cooled inverters failed on four out of the eight buses. These failures were attributed to the winter damp and summer dust that characterise the climatic conditions in Ferrara. Accordingly, the manufacturers, ALTRA, decided to adopt liquid-cooled electronic devices for the next bus generation.

7.3.4 Petrol-electric hybrid buses in Aalborg, Denmark
     (after Alessandrini and Luca [7.3]).

Five DAB-Hybridbus 346 and 348 buses were evaluated between 1997 and 1998 in the Danish town of Aalborg. Unusual features of these buses were the choice of a gasoline rather than a diesel engine, and Ni-Cd batteries. These hybrids were operated 25% of the time in purely electric mode. Comparisons were made between these and conventional diesel buses. This comparison is handicapped by the inherently higher efficiency of the diesel engine and the different emissions characteristics. The type 348 buses showed lower levels of emissions in all categories, but a 37.5% *greater* fuel consumption. Some of this increase can be attributed to the lower inherent efficiency of the petrol engine, and part may be related to the requirement for a large proportion of pure electric traction, but clearly the overall system efficiency was poor. Availability was very poor at 40%, and surprisingly, the vehicles were criticised for high levels of noise and vibration. A hybrid, especially a petrol-engined version, should be inherently quieter and smoother. This suggests that there were several unsatisfactory aspects of the design of the Aalborg buses. Fortunately, experience of hybrid buses in Brazil has been much more encouraging, as described below.

7.3.5 Battery-electric hybrid bus trials in Brazil (after Silva [7.4])

Experiences with hybrid battery-electric buses in Brazil have been much more positive than in the examples described above. Brazil has the fifth largest population in the world, with 170 million inhabitants, and two of the most populated cities: São Paulo with 17 million people and Rio de Janeiro with 10 million. The demand for public transport is enormous, and although there is some use of trains, light rail vehicles and trolleybuses, it is met largely by some 120,000 diesel buses. Understandably, the emissions problem in the major cities is a cause for concern. Hybrid buses are seen as providing potentially the best short to medium-term solution. Their main advantage compared to light rail, is the lower infrastructure costs. Brazil also has a strong automotive industry with many major engine and vehicle manufacturers operating plants in the country. There are also bus body manufacturers such as Marcopolo and Busscar.

To meet the challenge of producing viable and effective hybrid buses, a team of specialists was put together, with the specific purpose of developing hybrid traction systems for three types of vehicle.

1. Large 18 m long articulated bus with a maximum capacity of 170 passengers
2. Standard 12 m long vehicle for 105 passengers known as the 'Padron'
3. Microbuses 8 m long for 24 seated passengers.

The programme started with the development of the largest vehicle, the 18 m articulated bus shown in figure 7.11.

Figure 7.11: The Brazilian 18 m Eletra hybrid diesel-battery bus. (Photo courtesy of Eletra.)

Figure 7.12:   The 12 m hybrid diesel electric Eletra Padron bus.
(Photo courtesy of Eletra.)

The prototype has been in regular service for two and a half years at the time of writing, and more recently three of the regular sized Padron vehicles shown in figure 7.12 have entered service. The smaller vehicle started operating in October 2001. Following the technical success and good operational experience, the company 'Eletra' was formed for the purpose of manufacturing these buses to meet Brazilian trolleybus standards.

Technical description of the Brazilian buses (after Silva [7.4])

Architecture	hybrid series electrical with regenerative braking
Energy storage	sealed lead-acid batteries. The Padron used four battery boxes, with a total mass of 600 kg
Power transmission	alternatives of DC motor driven by IGBT chopper, or AC induction motor powered by IGBT variable frequency inverter
Prime-mover	diesel engine and brushless alternator

Measurements were made both during the development stage and later in regular operation. The results below are based on two and a half years of operation with the 18 m model, and one year with the 12 m Padron.

Results of trials

Emissions, noise levels and fuel consumption were compared with conventional diesel buses on the same routes. The relative reductions are shown in figure 7.13. The comparative reduction in emissions is in most cases extremely good. Even the NOx emissions are significantly lower. The most striking feature is the markedly reduced fuel consumption: an outcome that contrasts with the results of the Italian and Danish trials described above.

	Reduction relative to conventional diesel bus
Particulates	Better than 90%
Hydrocarbons and CO	60% to 70%
NOx	25% to 30%
Noise	Reduced to 65 db inside, compared to 85 db on conventional bus
Fuel consumption	10% to 25% depending on route, profile and average speed.

Figure 7.13: Comparisons between hybrid and conventional diesel buses (after Silva [7.4]).

The reliability of the vehicles has been good. It was initially estimated that the battery life would be around three years, and after two and a half years the original batteries are still performing well. This is again in marked contrast to the European results, and suggests that the Brazilian system was better optimised at the outset. Additional relative advantages of the hybrid system are listed below:

1. Brake lining life up to three times longer than for conventional buses.
2. Lower engine maintenance costs because of smaller engine and lower wear due to running at more constant speed.
3. Lower consumption of lubricating oil due to smaller size of engine.
4. Elimination of maintenance costs associated with the automatic transmission used on the conventional buses.

Operating experience indicates that monthly maintenance costs of hybrid buses is equal to or lower than that of conventional buses. The quietness and smoothness of operation are also attractive features. It seems from this experience that well designed and optimised hybrid battery-electric buses do show considerable advantages relative to conventional diesel vehicles, and that reliability can be comparable. The choice of battery design also seems to be critical to the success of the vehicles.

7.3.6 Battery-electric hybrid buses in Berlin (after Eberwein [7.5])

The Berliner Verkehrsbetriebe (BVG) has been running experimental hybrid diesel/battery-electric buses on an 8 km route to Tegel Airport (Berlin) since 1998. The buses run purely on battery-electric power for approximately 1.2 km in the immediate vicinity of the airport. The vehicle used was a 12 m Mercedes Benz bus with a pair of hub-mounted electric motors and a hybrid serial drive system. Technical details are as follows.

Generator	synchronous, continuous output 145 kW, max. 220 kW
Hub drive motors (2)	50 kW each, max. 75 kW
Batteries	51 MAXXIMA high-current lead-acid, 50 Ah 612 V, mounted in roof.

Two regulator systems are used. The characteristic curve regulator is responsible for the adjustment of the load at the generator, as well as the co-ordination of the amount of fuel injected into the i.c. engine. A capacity/power split regulator distributes the power between the battery and generator, and controls the battery charge/discharge rate. Three different control strategies were evaluated.

In the first, the vehicle is run effectively with simple diesel-electric transmission. The second strategy involved running the diesel continuously except in some pure battery zero emission phases. The i.c. engine operates on the characteristic curve for minimal energy consumption. The maximum generator output is limited to 100 kW: the most efficient level. The battery provides a boost for acceleration and also absorbs energy in regenerative braking.

The third strategy involves running the diesel engine on its most efficient characteristic curve, and simply switching off when little or no drive power is needed. Fuel savings of up to 15% were achieved, and with this strategy the batteries operated reliably with an estimated life of four years to replacement.

7.3.7 Conclusions from the diesel/battery-electric bus trials

The fact that both the Brazilian and Berlin buses were able to operate reliably, and produce fuel savings of around 15%, shows that with appropriate design and control systems, hybrid buses do offer low emissions and high efficiency. Despite the cost of replacing the batteries from time to time, the more successful designs have shown reductions in operating costs. In the case of the Berlin bus, a saving of 6000 DM over an eight year period is estimated. The fact that a 15% improvement compared to pure diesel vehicles has been achieved, shows the potential of the hybrid concept, since an electric transmission is inherently less efficient than a purely mechanical one. Some idea of the penalty imposed by electric transmission is provided by results of tests on some non-hybrid diesel/electric buses in Stuttgart, as described by Alessandrini and Luca [7.3].

The Stuttgart public transport company started to run a number of diesel electric buses in 1997. The fleet included seventeen 18 m long articulated types and two 12 m non-articulated. The purpose of using this form of transmission was that it produces smoother driving conditions and can accommodate a very low (kerb-height) floor. Comparisons between the diesel-electric vehicle and a conventional diesel bus carrying a similar load showed that the fuel consumption of the electric transmission vehicles was some 30% higher than that of the conventional bus. However, 15% of this difference was due to the installation of air-conditioning on the diesel-electric vehicles, 13% was due to the increased weight of the electric transmission system, and surprisingly only 2% was due directly to the lower transmission efficiency.

From this it will be observed that despite the natural handicap of high battery mass and reduced transmission efficiency, the hybrid diesel-electric bus can produce fuel savings in addition to significantly reduced emissions.

7.4 Flywheel hybrid vehicles

Batteries have an inherent weakness as storage devices. This includes their poor cycle life and storage efficiency, and a low specific power on recharge. In order to achieve a reasonable service life with brake energy recovery, only about 10% of the battery capacity can be used, so the installed battery has to be grossly oversized in terms of the required energy storage capacity. This leads to high weight and high capital cost. An attractive alternative is the flywheel, which can be charged or discharged at a very high power with no ill effects.

Objections to the flywheel are often based on an intuitive, but misplaced, fear of the possibility of failure of containment if the flywheel should break up. As described in Chapter 3, extensive testing has indicated that these fears are unfounded, at least in respect of conventional flywheels running at speeds of less than 50,000 rpm. There have been reports of dramatic failures of experimental 'ultraflywheels' running at speeds up to 300,000 rpm, but no devices of this type have yet been used in automotive applications. Apart from genuine safety concerns associated with any new technological development, there are strong commercial reasons why the battery manufacturers would wish to discourage development of the flywheel.

7.4.1 The Oerlikon Gyrobus

In Europe, there has been a significant amount of development and evaluation of flywheel-based hybrid vehicles, including buses, trolleybuses, and light rail vehicles. Probably the most well known early application of flywheel energy storage was in the Oerlikon Gyrobus, which was mentioned in Chapter 2, and is illustrated in figure 7.14. This vehicle was developed in the 1950s as a semi-autonomous version of the trolleybus, which was already in wide use in public transport. Conventional trolleybuses require a continuous overhead electrical supply in the form of a pair of wires supported by columns.

Figure 7.14:   The Oerlikon mains-electric/flywheel Gyrobus. The flywheel
                was recharged at each stop, and provided electrical propulsion
                between stops. (Photo courtesy of Frans Thoolen.)

    Apart from being unsightly, these wires and their supports are costly to install
and maintain. The system can also result in route inflexibility and there are
operational problems in the case of vehicle breakdown.
    By installation of a large flywheel energy store, the Gyrobus could store
sufficient energy to power the vehicle at full performance for a distance of
perhaps 1-2 km. This meant that continuous electrification was not necessary.
The flywheel was charged up rapidly at each stop through an overhead 3 phase
supply linked to an induction motor, which spun up the flywheel, normally in the
time it took to load and unload passengers. The vehicle could then be driven
under its own power to the next stop, by transmitting power electrically from the
flywheel to the traction motors. The performance was similar to that of a
conventional trolleybus and these vehicles operated successfully in the 1950s in
the city of Ghent, and then in Kinshasa (then Leopoldsville) in Africa. The
demise came with the phasing out of trolleybuses generally, as the diesel bus
became favoured among operators, though not necessarily among passengers.
Because of the current concerns over city centre emissions, and dissatisfaction
with diesel buses amongst the travelling public, there is now widespread interest
in bringing back buses with the performance and ride quality of trolleybuses;
hence the interest in hybrid propulsion for buses.

7.4.2 The Parry flywheel hybrid vehicles

Drawing on the experience of the Oerlikon bus, a series of small trams and light rail vehicles was developed by Parry People Movers of Cradley Heath, West Midlands, UK. A small early Parry rail vehicle, which was used to convey visitors around an entertainment park, is illustrated and described in Chapter 2. A larger later version is illustrated in figure 7.15. This later vehicle went into service on the Bristol Harbourside in 1997 to carry visitors from Prince Street Bridge near the Centre to the SS *Great Britain* [7.9]. This was the tenth of the flywheel-powered vehicles to be designed by John Parry and the first to go into fare-paying passenger service. It ran successfully for over two years and carried over 50,000 passengers. Both of these Parry vehicles had simple large steel flywheels that were charged from a low voltage supply at stops. The Bristol vehicle used a 72 V DC supply at track level under the platform at the stop. This took roughly 30 seconds, during which passengers embarked and paid their fare. Such a charging system was possible because the low voltage presented no danger to the public; the conductors were safe to touch. They were, however, disconnected when not charging the flywheel, as a further safety measure.

Figure 7.15: The Parry light tram or 'Railbus' No. 10 operating at Bristol Harbourside in 1999. (Photo Colin Jefferson.)

In these vehicles, power was transmitted from the flywheel to the drive via a mechanical variator, or continuously variable transmission (CVT). At the time, this was a novel application for the CVT and a novel form of drive for a tram.

Although CVTs are sometimes used in cars in place of gearboxes, the application here has the specific aim of extracting power from the flywheel in a controlled manner and, in theory, returning it during braking, by reversing the power flow. The efficiency of variators can be fairly high when the ratio is fixed, but when used to extract power from the flywheel with a varying ratio, the efficiency falls to between 70% and 50%. This means that the storage efficiency of the flywheel variator system could be as low as 20% to 25%. Part of this poor storage efficiency was due to the losses in the flywheel due to windage. Such losses are avoided on the more advanced flywheel systems described later, by containing the flywheel within a near vacuum. In the vehicle, shown in figure 7.15, a reasonably high overall energy efficiency was obtained mainly from the use of steel wheels and from the fact the vehicle speed was relatively low, as it ran through pedestrian areas.

With regard to safety concerns, it may be noted that the Parry vehicle described above had a steel flywheel and containment. The flywheel was never operated at more than half the safe speed defined by the British Standard for steel wheels. The vehicle was approved by the Health and Safety Executive and had a perfect safety record during its operation.

7.4.3 Experience with hybrid buses using diesel-engine/flywheel systems developed by Magnet Motor GmbH (after Reiner and Weck [7.6])

The Magnet Motor Company has developed a flywheel storage system called 'Magnetodynamic Storage' (MDS) which has been evaluated extensively in trials of both diesel/electric and trolley buses. The original K3 units had a storage capacity of 2 kWh (7.2 MJ) and a power output of 150 kW.

The MDS flywheel system is compact, and uses a rotor in the form of a hollow cylinder, made primarily of carbon fibre compound. The motor/generator unit is integral with the rotor and employs permanent magnet excitation. Specially developed IGBT converters are used, and the unit is claimed to have an overall transmission efficiency of 91-95%, including the inverters. The rotating components are completely contained within a vacuum housing, which results in very low windage losses. The only system interface is electrical; there are no external mechanical connections. The vacuum is maintained by a small intermittently operated pump. Losses through friction in the mechanical roller bearings are minimised by the use of magnetic support for the rotor. The stator and inverters are liquid cooled. To avoid gyroscopic effects, the units are arranged with their rotational axis vertical, and are mounted within a gimballed cardanic frame, which may be seen in figure 7.19. Figure 7.16 shows the key data for the current range of MDS units.

In a public service vehicle, safety is a major concern, and the MDS unit meets all official safety requirements including a crash test at 6 g. Flywheels have a

		MDS K3	MDS K6	MDS M1
Energy storage	MJ	7.2	21.6	32.4
Specific energy	KJ/kg	18	55	55
Max. power	W	150	450	900
Specific power	kW/kg	.38	1.13	1.5
Operating speed	rpm	12 000	21 000	18 000
Diameter	m	0.66	0.66	0.78
Height	m	0.64	0.64	0.75
Mass	kg	400	400	600

Figure 7.16:   Technical data for the MDS flywheel units (after Reiner and Weck [7.6]).

much higher cycle life than any current type of battery. The lifetime of the MDS units is expected to be over 10^7 cycles, and it is estimated that for use in city buses, around 18,000 cycles per year will be required, so the flywheel units should comfortably outlive the vehicles.

Several Neoplan N4114DES buses were fitted with MDS K3 units and tested operationally in Munich and Bremen. As shown in Figure 7.17, two MM electric motors were mounted directly on the rear wheels via single-stage planetary gearing.

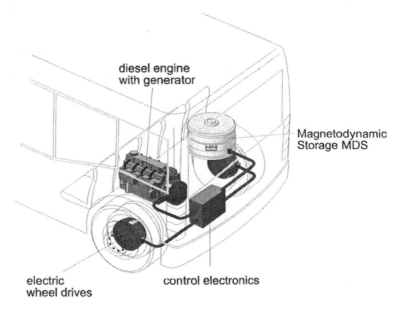

diesel engine with generator

Magnetodynamic Storage MDS

electric wheel drives

control electronics

Figure 7.17:   Arrangement of components in the Neoplan diesel/electric-flywheel bus. (Illustration courtesy of Magnet Motor GmbH.)

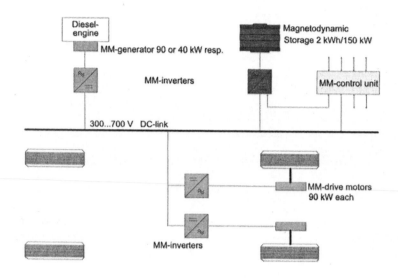

Figure 7.18:   The drive system in the MM hybrid bus.
(Illustration courtesy of Magnet Motor GmbH.)

These motors not only propel the vehicle, but provide electric braking. The prime mover was a Magnet Motor generator with a rating of 90 kW coupled directly to the output from a rear-mounted diesel engine. The MDS flywheel unit is also mounted at the rear on one side. The drive motors, generator and MDS unit are controlled by current inverters with IGBT power modules, as illustrated in figure 7.18. The buses have been operated in Munich and Bremen. The Bremen bus is shown in figure 7.19.

The performance of the hybrid buses in terms of fuel consumption was compared with that of diesel buses operating on the same route. An interesting feature of the results was that the performance of the hybrid buses was found to be relatively insensitive to the load carried. The effect of this was to produce high fuel savings of around 30% during the rush hour, but little or no gain during off-peak times. The overall daily improvement was 12%. From the results, it was estimated that with a fleet of 550 hybrid urban buses in daily service in Munich, the annual fuel savings would amount to 1.7 million litres.

Apart from the significant savings in fuel consumption, average emissions were also greatly reduced as shown in figure 7.20. The saving in CO_2 emissions directly reflects the reduction in fuel consumption.

Figure 7.19: The Magnet Motor-Neoplan flywheel bus as operated in Bremen. (Photo courtesy of Magnet Motor GmbH.)

Pollutant	Average change relative to a standard diesel bus
CO_2	−12%
CO	−50%
NOx	0%
Particulates	−49%

Figure 7.20: Average percentage reduction in emissions relative to a standard diesel bus (after Reiner and Weck [7.6]).

7.4.4 The Magnet Motor flywheel trolleybus

Twelve flywheel trolleybuses incorporating the Magnet Motor MDS energy storage units have been extensively evaluated in service in Basel, commencing in 1992. The purpose was to reduce the demand of each vehicle on the supply and thus increase the capacity of the line. The vehicle is illustrated in figure 2.8 (Chapter 2). Energy savings of between 20 and 25% relative to conventional trolleybuses on the same line have been achieved, this saving being almost entirely attributable to the effects of regenerative braking which is not usually possible with a standard trolleybus.

The prototype has now logged over 25,000 hours, and the total mileage of the buses is over 3.5 million kilometres. After some initial teething troubles, reliability of the MDS units is now excellent. With improved bearing design only one repair has been necessary in 38,000 hours of operation. For the power electronics, the estimated mean time between failures is estimated as 40,000 hours.

New flywheel designs have increased the power density by a factor of three, and Magnet Motor have suggested that two of the larger MDS K6 units could be integrated to act as the whole on-road energy source, with the units being recharged at the final stops. This would give a range of around 10 km.

7.4.5 The CCM flywheel energy storage systems

CCM (Centre for Construction and Mechatronics) is an independent technical research and development company who have developed a range of flywheel units for use in bus, trolleybus and light rail applications [7.7], [7.8]. The mechanical arrangements of the flywheel units are broadly similar to those of the Magnet Motor machines. Composite flywheel discs are used with a hollow steel rotor containing permanent magnets. The flywheel runs in a vacuum in a strong housing, which provides safety containment. The axis of rotation is vertical, and cardanic suspension is used. For road vehicles, a 200 kW unit has been developed with 2 kWh (7.6 MJ) effective storage capacity. The unit has been assessed in a converted trolleybus, as shown in figure 7.21. This bus, known as the 'Flywheel bus' has been demonstrated in service in the city of Eindhoven, Netherlands. It has been certified for operational safety and passenger carrying duty by the regulatory authorities. The prime mover was a 2 litre Audi engine/generator set that could be run on petrol or LPG.

Because of concerns expressed about the safety of flywheels, CCM have undertaken a great deal of work to ensure the safety of the devices. The flywheels have been tested at twice their specified speed without failure and have been demonstrated to be failsafe. These safety tests are described more fully in Chapter 3. Stringent safety protection is also applied to the electrical systems. In addition to these essentially passive safety arrangements, the units have an active monitoring system, which checks on speed, temperature, vibrations, voltage and current, and provides automatic shutdown if out of range operation is detected.

Figure 7.21: The CCM hybrid flywheel bus.

Because of the more or less maintenance free operation, the flywheel unit has demonstrated a virtually indefinite cycle life. The case for the use of flywheels as the energy storage element in hybrid passenger transit vehicles is thus almost proven, assuming that the fuel savings, emission reduction and lower maintenance costs justify the rather higher cost relative to batteries.

CCM have developed a more powerful 300 kW unit for application to larger vehicles. The storage capacity has been increased to 4 kWh by increasing the maximum speed. A geometrically smaller version is now under development for standard buses (200 kW × 2 kWh) that will be able to be mounted under the floor. Further developments using the CCM units are described below.

7.4.6 Some future bus developments

Figure 7.22 shows a production prototype hybrid bus developed by Irisbus, named the CIVIS, and designed for the commercial market. Though batteries are proposed for energy storage, a flywheel version is under consideration. Other options include a guided hybrid trolleybus.

Figure 7.22: The CIVIS hybrid bus. (Photo courtesy of CCM.)

The transport authorities in the Eindhoven region of the Netherlands are proposing to develop a rapid transit system linking the city with outer suburbs and the airport. A guided articulated bus has been chosen as the vehicle and hybrid propulsion has been proposed. In order to evaluate both the battery and flywheel energy storage systems, two prototypes have been built, one with each system. This will allow a comparison of the performance and life cycle costs to be made. The flywheel version uses the CCM flywheel described earlier. The vehicle, named 'Phileas' is shown in figure 7.23. It is designed to have the same passenger appeal as a light rail vehicle, and thus has a similar appearance. The traction requirements will also be similar to those of a light rail vehicle, so the propulsion system would also be suitable to power autonomous light rail vehicles, as discussed below.

There is no doubt that the hybrid bus is coming of age, and we will see it introduced as an alternative to conventional diesel buses, offering a significant environmental improvement and lower operating costs. The low noise and low

Figure 7.23:   Phileas: The proposed hybrid passenger transit vehicle for
                Eindhoven. (Photo courtesy of APTS b.v.)

emissions make the hybrid bus more comparable with a trolleybus, but without
the cost and visual impact of the overhead supply wire system. The hybrid bus
represents the first major step in bus development for a decade, and also
establishes hybrid propulsion as the way ahead for modern public transport
vehicle design.

7.5 Trams and light rail vehicles

The flywheel hybrid systems developed for buses are equally suitable for rail
vehicles and since, in urban use, brake energy represents a high proportion of
energy used, there is considerable scope for energy recovery and fuel savings. A
further advantage is that because few large gradients are involved in rail systems,
there is less need for cardanic suspension of the flywheel.

7.5.1 Development of the Parry rail vehicles

The operation of the Parry Railbus in Bristol was limited to routes with frequent
stops to allow for flywheel recharging. The range of the vehicle on one flywheel
charge was about 2 km. The vehicle also carried batteries so that it could be

operated as a battery/flywheel-electric hybrid, or on batteries only.   This extended its range somewhat, but the facility was really only intended for emergencies, if the flywheel energy should become depleted en route.   By addition of a small generator set, the vehicle range could be extended indefinitely, and in a subsequent development by Parry People Movers, a 25 kW gas engine powered generator set has been incorporated, to maintain the flywheel charge, in a series hybrid arrangement.   In a further proposal for a fuel cell/flywheel version of the vehicle, it has been estimated that a 12 kW fuel cell would be sufficient to maintain a service speed of 30 km/h on a level track.

7.5.2 The ULEV-TAP tram

In 1997 a project called 'Ultra Low Emission Vehicle - Transport with Advanced Propulsion', (ULEV-TAP) [7.10], received European Community funding and work commenced to design, build and test a gas turbine/flywheel hybrid system for a 30 ton light rail vehicle. The vehicle used for demonstration purposes was based on a refurbished ex-service conventional electric tram from Karlsruhe, as shown in figure 7.24. A gas turbine powered high-speed generator set of 70 kW power was developed for this project. The energy storage unit was a 300 kW CCM flywheel system of 4 kWh capacity, and a 220 kW drive/brake unit was employed with the original traction motors.

Figure 7.24:   The ULEV-TAP experimental light rail vehicle designed for gas turbine power.

Theoretical estimates indicated that a 90% reduction in noxious emissions and a 30% fuel saving compared to a conventional diesel-powered vehicle should be possible. At the end of the project, the vehicle, shown in figure 7.24, was demonstrated at the Alstom DDF test site in Reichshoffen, Alsace, over a 1 km test track. It was unfortunate that, in this demonstration, the gas turbine alternator system could not be operated for technical reasons, even though the two components had been satisfactorily tested individually. The demonstration was, however, carried out by charging the flywheel from an external source while the vehicle was stationary. The performance of the vehicle running just on flywheel power, was equal to that of the original vehicle, and was limited only by the original traction package. Brake energy recovery was also demonstrated to be satisfactory, again limited by the traction package. It was estimated by computer prediction, borne out by the trials, that an engine power of only 60 kW would be sufficient to maintain the performance of the vehicle on a typical Karlsruhe tram route.

The purpose of the project was partly to evaluate the gas turbine alternator system as the prime mover. The advantages of the vehicle include the potential compactness and low maintenance cost, and the ability to run on a variety of fuels, including diesel, with very low emissions. The project proved the concept, and it is expected that a follow-on project will be undertaken, to build a production prototype for rail applications. The choice of prime mover will probably be up to the end user, but in the longer term, the fuel cell could be a strong candidate where silent pollution-free operation is required. This could indeed make electrification of passenger transit routes an obsolete requirement. Further information on this project is available from reference [7.10].

7.6 In conclusion

The effectiveness and advantages of hybrid propulsion systems have been demonstrated for a variety of types of public transport vehicles. Compared to conventional diesel buses, hybrid vehicles can have significantly higher efficiency, and produce a much lower level of noxious emissions. They also have most of the advantages of electric vehicles without the need for unsightly overhead conductor wires, which are expensive to install and maintain. Such advantages include low noise, smooth stepless transmission, and the ability to accommodate low flat flooring.

As with any new technology, it will take some time to overcome the natural ⟵ caution of operators, particularly as the capital cost of the new vehicles is likely to be initially higher than that of conventional mass-produced alternatives. Municipal authorities have sometimes hampered the introduction of these new vehicles. Other reasons for the slow introduction are that diesel fuel is still relatively cheap, and that emissions regulations are generally not yet so stringent as to absolutely necessitate a move away from conventional i.c. engines, particularly now that technological advances have reduced their emissions considerably. The improved fuel efficiency has however spurred the introduction of hybrid vehicles in South America where fuel costs are high, and the supply of oil is insecure. There has also been great interest in the hybrid vehicle in Italy where it is seen as a means of reducing the damaging effects of pollution in crowded medieval towns.

For passenger cars, the introduction of 36/42 V electrical systems is likely to encourage the development of mild hybrid propulsion systems with attendant improvements in fuel efficiency and reductions in emissions. Toyota and Honda seem keen to press ahead with the introduction and further development of their hybrid vehicle technologies. Other manufacturers have shown more caution in introducing hybrid cars but some, such as Audi, have produced convincing development models, and are thus in a good position to rise to the challenge if or when this becomes necessary.

There currently seems to be a widespread belief that fuel cells will become the preferred prime-mover for land transport. However, the problems of hydrogen distribution and the environmental implications of hydrogen production do not appear to have been fully appreciate. If the fuel cell does emerge as a major form of prime-mover, then it is likely that fuel cell vehicles will employ hybrid propulsion systems in order to increase the efficiency and to improve the responsiveness to power demand. In short, hybrid propulsion systems are likely to be used increasingly, and in a wide variety of vehicles.

7.7 References

[7.1]   Bursa, Mark, Toyota's double-drive hybrid powertrain, *ISATA Magazine*, May 1997.
[7.2]   Dettmer, Roger, Hybrid vigour, *IEE Review*, January 2001.
[7.3]   Alessandrini, Adriano and Luca, Persia, Evaluation of hybrid buses in urban public transport service, *Proceedings of the Prosper Congress*, Karlsruhe, September 2001, www.prosper.ttk.de
[7.4]   Silva, Antonio Vicente S., Hybrid buses: the Brazilian experience, *Proceedings of the Prosper Congress*, Karlsruhe, September 2001, www.prosper.ttk.de
[7.5]   Eberwein, Bukhard, Hybridbus experience of the BVG, *Proceedings of the Prosper Congress*, Karlsruhe, September 2001, www.prosper.ttk.de
[7.6]   Reiner, Gerhard and Weck, Werner, Twelve years of experience with MDS flywheel storage systems in urban transport buses, *Proceedings of the Prosper Congress*, Karlsruhe, September 2001, www.prosper.ttk.de
[7.7]   Smits, E., Huisman, H. and Thoolen, F., A hybrid city bus using an electro mechanical accumulator for power demand smoothing, *Proceedings of the European Power Electronics Conference*, Vol. 4, Trondheim, 1997.
[7.8]   Huisman, H., Smits, E. J. F. M. and Veltman A., 'Control design for a hybrid city bus', *Proceedings of the European Power Electronics Conference*, Vol. 4, Trondheim, 1997, EPE-99, Lausanne, 1999.

[7.9] Ackerman, M. C., Davies, T. S., Jefferson, C. M., Marquez, J. M. and Skinner, J., Transport needs of the city of tomorrow, *Proceedings Urban Transport VI*, pp. 3-12, Cambridge, July 2000. Eds. Sucharov, L. and Brebbia, L., WIT Press, Southampton, ISBN 1 85312 823 6.

[7.10] Etemad , S., Thoolen, F. and Berndt, J., *Proceedings of the Prosper Congress*, Karlsruhe, September 2001, www.prosper.ttk.de

INDEX

Modelling Urban Vehicle Emissions

M. KHARE, *Indian Institute of Technology, India* and **P. SHARMA**, *Indraprastha University, India*

Vehicular air pollution poses the main threat to urban air quality and is therefore one of the major components of urban air quality studies. Air quality models can play an effective role in the efficient management of such pollution.

This unique book presents various air quality modelling techniques, previously scattered throughout the literature, together with their applications. Comprehensive and well-organised, it also provides a step-by-step guide to using these models, followed by case studies to illustrate the points discussed. A methodology for formulating a local air quality management programme, including a discussion of the significance of different air quality models, is also featured.

Partial Contents: Urban Air Quality Management and Modelling; Air Pollution Due to Vehicular Exhaust Emissions - A Review; Development of Vehicular Exhaust Models; Application of Vehicular Exhaust Models.

Series: Advances in Transport, Vol 9

ISBN: 1-85312-897-X
2002   232pp
£79.00/US$123.00/€129.00

Innovations in Freight Transport

Editors: **E. TANIGUCHI**, *Kyoto University, Japan* and **R.G. THOMPSON**, *University of Melbourne, Australia*

Intelligent Transport Systems (ITS), such as advanced information systems, automatic vehicle identification systems, and global positioning systems, have recently been developed and deployed achieving improvements in cost reduction, better service to customers, and traffic congestion. Illustrating recent progress in the subject, this title also highlights innovative concepts for the management of logistics systems.

Contents: Introduction; Intelligent Transport Systems I; Intelligent Transport Systems II; Vehicle Routing and Scheduling Problems; Logistics Terminals; Intermodal Freight Transport; Transport Demand Management; New Freight Transport Systems; Economic Perspectives; Supply Chain Management; E-Commerce; Future Perspectives.

Series: Advances in Transport, Vol 11

ISBN: 1-85312-894-5
2002   apx 264pp
apx £89.00/US$138.00/€145.00

Practical Applications of Design Optimization

S. HERNÁNDEZ and A.N. FONTÁN PÉREZ, Universidad de La Coruña, Spain

The scientific field of design optimization has evolved tremendously both in terms of theory and of the software available to support it.

Based on a recent research project, this essentially practical text provides a thorough introduction to the current applications of design optimization. The authors also apply its principles to some branches of engineering for the first time. The methodology is fairly general and can be applied to many real-life engineering problems in fields as diverse as architecture and automobiles.

Written for engineers whose work is related to design, the book will also be of interest to postgraduate students and lecturers dealing with design optimization. An accompanying CD-ROM contains related programs.

Contents: Origin of the Techniques of Design Optimization; Current State of Optimization Techniques; Laminated Steel Shapes; Mechanical Elements for Automobiles; Prestressed Concrete Beams; Aluminium Structural Bars; Vehicle Chassis; Future Developments in Optimum Design Technology.

Series: High Performance Structures and Materials, Vol 3

ISBN: 1-85312-886-4
2002   240pp + CD-ROM
£98.00/US$148.00/€156.00

Ekranoplanes
Controlled Flight Close to the Sea

A. NEBYLOV, St Petersburg State University, Russia and P.A. WILSON, University of Southampton, UK

This book is dedicated to the problem of flight control over the sea at low altitudes, and is concerned particularly with Ekranoplanes.

Translated from the original Russian, it will be of great interest to specialists in aviation and marine instrumentation, and to researchers and designers of control systems for ekranoplanes, hovercraft, hydrofoils, helicopters, special purpose aircraft, search-and-rescue craft and other types of transport designed for motion close to the sea. A video on CD-ROM showing various versions of the Ekranoplane in flight and general operation is included.

Contents: Transport Vehicles for Motion Close to Supporting Surfaces; Principles of Construction of Low Altitude Flight Sensor Parameters; Sea Waves' Probability Characteristics in Space and Time; Sea Roughness Characteristics in Moving Frame; Characteristics of Errors of Low Altitude Flight Parameters Sensors; Synthesis of Integrated Systems for Measuring Motion Parameters; Examples of Integrated Meters Synthesis; Integrated Meters Investigation Under Instability Conditions of Operating and Possible Sensor Failures; Digital Realization of Integration Algorithms.

ISBN: 1-85312-831-7
2002   apx 250pp + video on CD-ROM
apx £225.00/US$348.00/€365.00

Computers in Railways VIII

Editors: **J. ALLAN**, *Railway Safety, UK,* **E. ANDERSSON**, *KTH Railway Technology, Sweden,* **C.A. BREBBIA**, *Wessex Institute of Technology, UK,* **R. J. HILL**, *Consultant, UK,* **G. SCIUTTO**, *University degli Studi di Genova, Italy and* **S. SONE**, *University of Kogakuin, Japan*

This volume features the proceedings of the Eighth International Conference on Computer Aided Design, Manufacture and Operation in the Railway and other Advanced Mass Transit Systems (COMPRAIL).
Invaluable to railway managers, consultants, railway engineers (including signal and control engineers), designers of advanced train systems and computer specialists, the proceedings include sections covering: Advanced Train Control Systems; Infrastructure; Systems Engineering and Safety; Planning; Electromagnetic Compatibility; Scheduling and Crew Rostering; Freight Traffic and Passenger Interface; Energy Management and Power Supply; Traction and Maglev and Linear Mechanics; Rail-Wheel Dynamics and Pantograph and Catenary Interaction; Vehicle Dynamics and Fatigue; Traffic Control; Maintenance and Condition Monitoring; Multi-Train Simulators; Training, Decision Support and Human Interface Systems; Control Systems and Communication; Train Location Systems.
Series: Advances in Transport, Vol 13

ISBN: 1-85312-913-5
2002   1200pp
£324.00/US$499.00/€527.31

Air Pollution X

Editors: **C.A. BREBBIA**, *Wessex Institute of Technology, UK and* **J.F. MARTIN-DUQUE**, *Universidad Complutense, Spain*

Bringing together recent results and state-of-the-art contributions from researchers around the world, this book contains papers first presented at the Tenth International Conference on the Modelling, Monitoring and Management of Air Pollution. Emphasis is placed on the development of experimental and computational techniques, which can be used as tools to aid solution and understanding of practical air pollution problems.
Scientists working in industry, research organisations, government and academia, on the monitoring, simulation and management of air pollution problems will find this book invaluable.
Contents: Air Pollution Modelling; Air Quality Management; Urban Air Pollution; Urban and Suburban Transport Emissions; Monitoring and Laboratory Studies; Global Studies; Comparison of Modelling with Experiments; Indoor Pollution; Pollution Engineering; Fluid Mechanics for Enviromental Problems; Chemistry of Air Pollution; Aerosols and Particles; Health Problems; Chemical Transformation Modelling; Emission Inventories; Indoor Pollution.
Series: Advances in Air Pollution, Vol 11

ISBN: 1-85312-916-X
2002   apx 650pp
apx £214.00/US$332.00/€348.00